P9-DFR-896

THE
WISDOM
OF
MORRIE

BOOKS BY MORRIE SCHWARTZ

The Wisdom of Morrie (with Rob Schwartz)

Letting Go: Reflections on Living While Dying
(rereleased as *Morrie: In His Own Words*)

The Nuclear Seduction (with others)

Social Approaches to Mental Patient Care
(with Charlotte Schwartz)

The Nurse and the Mental Patient
(with E. L. Shockley)

The Mental Hospital (with Alfred Stanton)

The
WISDOM
of
MORRIE

Living and Aging
Creatively and Joyfully

MORRIE SCHWARTZ

edited by Rob Schwartz

**BLACK
STONE**
PUBLISHING

Excerpts from "Do Not Go Gentle into That Good Night" by Dylan Thomas,
from *The Poems of Dylan Thomas* (New Directions, 2017), used by permission.

Excerpts from *The Collected Works of W. B. Yeats, Volume I: The Poems,
Revised* by W. B. Yeats, edited by Richard J. Finneran, reprinted with the
permission of Scribner, a division of Simon & Schuster, Inc. Copyright
© 1940 by Georgie Yeats, renewed 1968 by Bertha Georgie Yeats,
Michael Butler Yeats, and Anne Yeats. All rights reserved.

Excerpts from "East Coker" and "Burnt Norton" from *Collected Poems,
1909–1962* by T. S. Eliot, used by permission of HarperCollins Publishers.
Copyright © 1963 by T. S. Eliot.

"With Age Wisdom" from *Collected Poems, 1917–1982* by Archibald MacLeish,
used by permission of HarperCollins Publishers. Copyright © 1985 by
The Estate of Archibald MacLeish.

Excerpt from "Courage" by Anne Sexton, reprinted by permission
of SLL/Sterling Lord Literistic, Inc. Copyright © by Anne Sexton,
c/o Linda Sexton, Literary Executor.

Printed in the United States of America

First edition: 2023
ISBN 979-8-200-81345-2
Self-Help / Motivational & Inspirational

Version 2

Blackstone Publishing
31 Mistletoe Rd.
Ashland, OR 97520

www.BlackstonePublishing.com

FOREWORD

I rediscovered this manuscript in the early 2000s, well after my dad had passed away. It was tucked in a desk drawer in his study, in our lovely house in Newtonville (the one with the maple tree in front). After much family discussion and consideration, we decided I should edit and take this writing to publication.

My dad believed this project would likely be his last mass contribution to help people. He had no inkling that *Tuesdays with Morrie* would come into existence. But those familiar with Mitch Albom's beautiful book will recognize the thoughts here. Dad was primarily concerned with improving people's lives. He set out to devise practical tips and techniques to help one age creatively, vibrantly, and joyfully.

I had the good fortune to sit with Dad and discuss all these ideas when he was writing the book (more on this in the afterword). It just so happened that in the spring and summer of 1989, I was at home after a long sojourn in Asia. Dad was formulating the project at the time and wrote the book during mid-1988 to mid-1992. We were able to explore in depth what he wanted to say, and this has been invaluable in bringing the project forward now.

One of my main focuses in editing was to keep my father's unique voice. The work is a blend of Dad's two communicating styles: academic and philosophical but at the same time down-to-earth, unassuming, and lovingly personal. I hope that distinctive amalgam has been preserved.

Pop was very prescient in perceiving orientations that would become more accepted decades later. He was interested in creating an environment where one's age doesn't influence how one is viewed by society. One of his primary concerns throughout his life was the psychological state of the individual. In much the same way as the Supreme Court observed in its landmark 1954 *Brown v. Board of Education* ruling, irreparable psychological harm is done to people who are made to feel excluded or somehow less than those in the dominant society. Dad saw how elderly or aging people had been made to feel less worthy than others, and he hoped this book would be part of a movement to correct that.

The psychological aspect (related to dad's professional and academic training) is the backdrop. He hoped to offer practical techniques to help people maintain an active and vibrant life. Some of the suggestions may feel familiar—the idea of using laughter, for instance (chapter four). It's a practice that many have written about more recently. Another concept that pervades these pages is Buddhist mindfulness.

The episodic nature of the book makes it both engaging and fun. Dad felt the real-life nature of the personal vignettes and episodes was the core of the book.

But this is a very different book from *Tuesdays with Morrie*, though an overarching humanitarianism and universal love run through both. Mitch's superb book is wonderfully concise and deals with the philosophical, societal, and personal values my father had. This book is more discursive. Dad provides many illustrations and stories to exemplify a point. In a way, the two volumes' differing approaches make them bookends for each other. I think Dad would be very happy about this because it reflects one of his favorite philosophical models: *the tension of opposites.*

It is a great pleasure for me to present Dad's ideas. This is the last great writing project he undertook before he got ill. In these pages, I hear his voice ringing throughout, sometimes as if we were back in his Newtonville study, discussing the insights. "There is no forced retirement from aging creatively."

—Rob Schwartz,
June 2021, Brookline, MA

INTRODUCTION

Later life is a special period of development, with unique limitations and opportunities. And it may be the most important phase of your life. You can change a lot in later life—if you really want to. For some, the process of getting older is a troublesome string of transitions. At times, it amounts to nothing less than a shattering of the things we took for granted. If you are preoccupied with your aging—alarmed by it, ashamed of it, discouraged or frightened by it—or if the change in identity forced on you is intolerable, you might find it difficult to concentrate on aging well. On the other hand, if you take your aging in stride and look at it as a challenging opportunity, you can use your attempts to grapple with the issues of aging as a vehicle for becoming the person you were meant to be.

Growing old is quintessentially human. If we're fortunate enough to survive middle age, we all will face certain inevitable experiences, both losses and opportunities. Beyond the particulars of our individual biographies, we each face certain common challenges and choices. Will we face our fear of death, or deny and try to avoid it? Will we still try to fulfill our deepest needs, or give up on them? Will we grow into wisdom, or sink into despair? Will we "go gentle into that good night," or will we hold on to life with every fiber, kicking at anything that would pull us away? Unlike in modern industrialized countries, where many view the elderly as redundant and obsolete, numerous cultures around the globe recognize the later years as a time of profound meaning, transformation, spirituality, and joy. I believe it is possible—and desirable—for us to do the same.

Lately, we see more and more articles and predictions in books, magazines, and the mass media suggesting a changing view toward the elderly: new ways of engaging with and "using" people in later life, and new anticipations that later life will be a time for achievement, excitement, and creativity. Abraham Heschel says old age can be regarded "not as the age of stagnation but as the age of opportunities for inner growth."[1]

There are many good reasons to believe that our

---

1 Abraham J. Heschel, *The Insecurity of Freedom* (New York: Farrar, Straus and Giroux, 1955), 78.

lives could culminate in some of the most meaningful, worthwhile, fulfilling activity we've ever undertaken. Almost daily, we see news stories or hear accounts of extraordinary achievements in later life. What's to stop us from developing new perspectives and seeking out new horizons, opening ourselves up to the unexpected, and finding new stimulation and a sharpened appetite for living fully? What's to stop us from enhancing the quality of our lives by achieving greater awareness, emotional depth, and self-respect? (Yes, even at our age.) We can shed light on the nature of who we are and who we might yet become, and what a more fulfilling existence might look like. We can believe in ourselves, have faith that we can change our lives in significant ways, and pursue goals we'd never envisioned. And we can believe, as Carl Jung's theory posits, "that the greatest potential for growth and self-realization exists in the second half of life."[2]

One of the best things about growing older is that no boss is looking over your shoulder, telling you what to do. Most of us have more control over our time now than ever before. And when we face new challenges,

---

2 Bruce Baker, MD and Jane Hollister Wheelwright, "Analysis with the Aged," in *Jungian Analysis*, ed. Murray Stein (La Salle, IL: Open Court, 1982), 256-274.

we encounter fewer external rewards or penalties, leaving us with only those that we give ourselves. We can, however, experience the inner satisfaction of choosing to create a life that reflects our reasonable and adventurous desires and aspirations, thus freeing ourselves from ageist assumptions that tell us we are finished, useless, and of little value. *There is no forced retirement from aging creatively.*

Now is the time to come to terms with old issues that are still dragging us down, to age well, and to become the best person we can be. I hope this book will help you do so in the best, most meaningful way for you. In these pages, I share with you the insights into aging I've collected over the past several years. My psychological and sociological knowledge, accrued over a forty-year career as a professor of sociology, and my understanding of human relations inform the work. So has the understanding I've acquired talking with friends and colleagues. This book draws on my work counseling people in later life, running psychotherapy groups focused on aging issues, keeping up with the popular and academic literature on aging, and reading autobiographies of older people. I also especially draw on my self-observations and reflections about my own aging, and my experiences of coming to terms with growing into my seventies.

I believe that trying to become the best person we

can be, aging well, and coming to terms with our issues might be the most important and meaningful goals to strive for in later life. We all can realize more of our potential by reaching for ideals that are not fully attainable. But in striving, we can learn how to live more effectively and with greater joy. And we can choose the life we wish to lead. I cannot provide a definitive plan, a path, or a specific set of procedures to follow in pursuit of your goals—your life is unique; a cookie cutter is not the tool to improve it. I will provide some ideas on how we might pursue the goals I have proposed. But in striving for your goals, you'll also discover your own ways to move forward.

This book is for everyone, though it may especially speak to people over sixty-five and retired, who are asking themselves, "What shall I do with the rest of my life?" It may be a useful platform for middle-aged people to preview what their future might look like. They will find much that is relevant to their current lives and also in their efforts to better understand and deal with their aging parents. The book is also for group facilitators in senior living centers and community homes, where it can kick-start group discussions of the opportunities, challenges, and dilemmas that arise in later life. Of course, no reader is too young to start looking ahead to their later years, or to profit from reading this book.

I also intend this book for readers with widely

varying backgrounds, which naturally affect how we age. For instance, someone who has never worked outside the home will experience their later years differently from a careerist whose company just hit them with mandatory retirement. Similarly, someone who dealt with a disability or serious illness in their youth will deal with aging differently from someone who experienced good health until their later years. Such differences influence how we age and what issues we will face in the process. When reading this book, pay attention to the ideas that speak to your experience and engage your imagination.

Every author loves a careful reader, and I'm no different. I urge you not to zip through this book. Take the time to think about an issue carefully, look at it from many sides, and talk about it, perhaps even in a discussion group. Talking with friends, peers, and family is crucial. You may benefit from keeping a journal of their thoughts and reactions. Allow the ideas the time and thought they deserve. This is a book for discovering more about yourself. It can help you reflect on your later life and its richness of opportunities. And it can help you change the attitudes and actions you want to change.

ONE

Awakening

I remember vividly my feelings on recognizing with a start that I was an older person: first the shudder, then the confusion, then the depression, then the sorting out, and then *finally* the stabilization and, mostly, acceptance.

I rarely had been ill before May 1984, when I was sixty-seven years old. I hadn't given much thought to illness, or aging, or the fact that the Social Security Administration officially labeled me "elderly." Nor did I in any way identify with the older generation. I quite unconsciously shared the ageist prejudice that to be old meant that you were in decline and "over the hill," and that old people were not to be admired. So who would want to be—or even be thought—"old"?

I taught at a university, where I was surrounded by young people and where most of my colleagues were much younger than I. With few exceptions my friends outside the university were also much younger—and

1

the exceptions themselves were vigorous and "young for their age." At the time, I was healthy, full of vitality, and actively involved in a variety of projects. I maintained a quiet pride in the fact that I looked and acted so much younger than I was. And the cardiologist telling me I had the arteries of a twenty-year-old only boosted my youthful self-concept. Thus, most of my life conspired to reinforce my "young" self-image and repress the fact that I was not far from my seventieth birthday. Such avoidance of the chronological facts meant that I'd given little thought to the issues I would inevitably encounter as I grew older. One could say I was an aging innocent and an innocent about aging—that I was a victim of our culture's adulation of youth and its disdain for "the old."

All this changed suddenly in the spring of 1984 when, *bang*, I began to suffer from severe asthma and had to have prostate surgery. I was not emotionally prepared for these maladies, one of which was heading into the chronic category, and the other being characteristic of older men. In one fell swoop, my body confronted me inescapably with my own aging and led to a crisis and eventual transformation in my identity. The painful recognition of my actual age and the vulnerabilities of aging overwhelmed and deeply distressed me.

I came to feel with some urgency that I needed to pull myself together and make clear to myself how I could do the most with the years left to me. I concluded that I would like to pursue the three goals indicated above—goals we can all benefit from adopting in these later years. I decided that to age well, I must try to keep myself in good physical shape. As a consequence, I began to swim regularly, paid attention to my diet and added some supplements, had a deep massage weekly, and undertook a course of acupuncture to reduce the effects of my asthma. On the psychological level, I tried to meditate regularly, paid closer and more caring attention to my family and friends, and set aside periods when I would relax and spend time with myself. I also tried to avoid noxious interpersonal relationships and situations. And finally, I came to see the importance of coming to terms with my fear of death.

Thus, illness precipitated a deepened awareness of my need to be alert to ways that I could improve the quality of my life while aging and coming to terms with ultimate existential issues.

So there I was at sixty-seven, aging in later life. The more I thought about it, the more I wondered about the misconceptions I carried in my head about older age. But asthma attacks frequently interrupted these ruminations. After an attack subsided, I would curse my fate and my vulnerabilities. I would fall into deep despair and rail against my body's betrayal. Depressed, I longed only to get back to how I was before I became ill. As my illness improved, I was content to coast along on my teaching, counseling, and psychotherapeutic work. To be "back to normal," relatively free of the struggle to breathe, doing what I had done for the past few decades, seemed a blessing. As my symptoms finally came under complete control, I became much freer of their constraints, and my expectations for the future soared. I became attracted to the idea of making my aging a creative activity, an adventure, and an opportunity to develop new skills, interests, and relationships as well as deepen old ones.

Undergoing the different phases of my illness had reinforced in me, in an emotionally powerful way, an awareness of illness's impact in shaping my feelings, ambitions, and identity. I noticed particularly how depressed and inactive I was in the first phase of my illness, when I had a guilty sense of myself as a useless person. And in the second phase, I had a mild awakening in which I could see myself coasting along with the tide and sometimes being more active. In the final phase, I felt I could be an enthusiastic and vital participant engaged in the stream of life. Having awakened to my aging, I could see possibilities for fulfilling unrealized potentials. And I began to pay more careful attention to my feelings and attitudes about getting older, and to record what was happening to me.

My illness had raised several important questions that I believe other people also ask in later life: How well or poorly will I age? How can I come to terms with my own death? And how can I remain hopeful and become a more positive human being?

Although struggling with asthma, I continued to teach at the university until my retirement at seventy, and I maintained my counseling practice. After retirement, I faced the question "What should I do with the rest of my life?" I didn't want to increase my clinical practice as my major activity, but I felt I needed a project that would energize me, enlist my enthusiasm, and challenge me. A friend suggested that writing a book about aging might both help me age well and help others at the same time. Here is that book . . .

Although in my life this upward turn of my spirits corresponded with improvements in my physical health, we certainly do not need to be in tip-top shape to grow, age well, and be the best person we can be. How much insufficient funds, illness, or a disability prevents us from aging well depends on the degree of poverty, the severity of the illness or disability, and the depth of determination of the individual. Apart from adversities at the extreme end, it's always possible to find ways to derive much satisfaction from living, as illustrated by this *Boston Globe* article from 1992[3]. It describes how a man of eighty-one, thanks to the depth of his determination, continued to grow and age well despite his disabilities, illnesses, and losses.

---

3 Gary Libman, "At 81, this graduate proves it's always possible to learn more," *Boston Globe*, July 19, 1992.

AT 81, THIS GRADUATE PROVES IT IS ALWAYS POSSIBLE TO LEARN MORE

At a ceremony attended by two of his children and three grandchildren, [Jacob] Blitzstein, 81, graduated from high school.

After Principal Lanny Nelms handed him the diploma and announced his age, Blitzstein waved to the audience and cried.

And why not? He's probably the oldest Central High graduate since the school opened in 1974. Although no records of such things are kept, a Los Angeles district spokesman says Blitzstein is the oldest graduate he's ever heard of.

Earning his diploma took 10 years, during which the retired store owner suffered a stroke and two bouts of pneumonia, had two pacemakers installed and lost his wife and two siblings.

He kept to his task for a reason. School "is the best medicine you can have," he says. "You have something on your mind—a goal."

Although he completed high school and some Jewish studies in his native Ukraine in the 1920s, Blitzstein says, "I had in my mind all the time that I still want to study.

"When you live in a nation like the US, which is the best experience in your life, you want to know the history. I read the newspapers, but it's not enough.

"So I went to high school with the idea it doesn't matter what happens, I have to get my diploma. I don't know if I'm going to be sick or die."

Blitzstein didn't die; he flourished under the demands for grades and papers. In his class of 89, he was one of two students who earned perfect 4.0 averages.

Although determined to get his degree, he sometimes has wavered under the burden of repeated illnesses.

"After my stroke, I had to reregister," he says. "My hand was shaking so badly I couldn't sign. I figured this was the time I had to get out.

"The counselor took my hand. She said, 'Jacob, it's nothing. Don't worry. I'll sign for you.'"

At the graduation ceremony, he was so excited that, while shaking hands with dignitaries onstage, he didn't realize fellow students were giving him a standing ovation. "My son told me later," he says.

Onstage, he did have the presence of mind to ask

what time it was. The school had tried to start the ceremony promptly at 6:30 p.m. so Blitzstein could return home by sundown to observe the Jewish Sabbath.

Blitzstein left right after the ceremony but not before about 10 students had asked to have their pictures taken with him . . .

With his diploma in hand, Blitzstein maintains that he's not through yet.

"You know something? I'm going to college," he told a visitor recently. He has checked out West Los Angeles and Santa Monica community colleges and says he hopes to transfer from there to a four-year school.

"It's not a joke," he says. "If I live to the year 2000, maybe I'll be a doctor."

FEAR OF AGING

Between the time I suffered my asthma attacks and the writing of this book, how I feared aging! I dreaded the uncertainty and unpredictability of the future. I anticipated pain, suffering, and dysfunctions, all from the same cause: growing older. I resented the negative attitudes and actions directed toward me because I was older.

When I met acquaintances after a thirty- or forty-year

interval, I was aghast and reacted internally with a rejecting shudder. I perceived them as shaky, without their
previous alertness or vitality, wrinkled, weak—old! Sometimes, I scarcely recognized them. I was saddened. I pitied
them and then wondered if they saw the same things in
me. In retrospect, I recognize that I avoided older people.
And when I had to interact with them, I actually felt a
slight distaste or uneasiness in their presence. Yet, I consider myself a tolerant and unprejudiced person.

So, too, for many of the people I talked with infor-
mally or in groups. The thought of being old or identified
with the "older population" also didn't fit them. When
I asked Jane, then seventy-five, when she first started
thinking of herself as old, she reacted indignantly, saying,
"I'm not old, and I don't think of myself as being old." To
her and many others, the term "old" had a bad conno-
tation, and they refused to "own it." They either denied
or disregarded their own moving into later life, believing it was not happening to them, but to others. Some
people tried to look and act young—men by engaging
in vigorous sports or hanging out with younger women,
and women by dyeing their hair or having cosmetic surgery. They had no interest in my suggestion that there
might be some value in defining themselves as seniors
or as "older people" and challenging themselves to fulfill their potential in later life. In this way, I got another
glimpse of the ageist attitudes that many of us older

people incorporate in our thinking and carry out in our actions.

The fact that people in later life have many stigmatizing attitudes toward older people and, therefore, toward ourselves should come as no surprise since ageist attitudes are so deep and strong, unconscious, and prevalent in our society. Much like other social subgroups, we internalize the ageist view so that many of us no longer expect, or are expected, to lead useful, productive, creative lives. This ageism can be every bit as debilitating as a disease.

By coming to terms with our ageism, we can learn to approve of ourselves, accept ourselves, and even love ourselves as older people. We can begin to see that the consequences of ageist attitudes and actions make older people feel more insecure, more uncertain, more ashamed, and less human. But we can feel worthy and worthwhile, not despite our age, but *because* of it—because of who we are as older people. Overcoming ageism brings that positive regard for ourselves, which makes it easier to challenge ageism wherever it rears its ugly head.

MOTIVATION

To rise to the challenges that come in later life, older people need strong sources of motivation. High motivation gives us the energy we need to pursue our goals in the face of ageism, loss, and illness. Motivation is the inspiration to act—an urge that generates effort and focused action. It is the push to try, to assert oneself, counteracting unwillingness, resistance, weariness, inertia, fear, and anxiety.

Some of us have a nearly endless supply of energy accompanying our high motivation. For others, the ability to keep on keeping on is unreliable: sometimes it's there, sometimes it isn't. Still others of us have a hard time mustering any motivation and are in a constant struggle to find meaning in what we are doing. For motivation and its accompanying energy to be present, flowing, and continuous, we must believe in the value of what we are doing.

Regardless of our usual level of motivation, we all have in us a vitality, a life energy, an urge to act, to live, and to feel some passion about others and the world. It is a force that can overcome resistance to doing those things we somehow find difficult or impossible to do. But our life energy may be locked in, just waiting to be liberated. It may be pushing to get out. But it's up to us to tap into that source of life energy within us. It's up to us to find ways to let it out, get it out, evoke it, coax it. To age well, we need to get in touch with this life energy, become familiar with it, nourish it, and invite it in as an enduring power in pursuing our goals and dreams.

And to discover the true nature of our motivation,

we need to be asking the right questions. What gets you excited to confront your tasks instead of avoiding them? What pushes you to try to understand your feelings and connect with others? What gets you to assume responsibility for a plan of action that you deem necessary or desirable, or to answer another's request for action? What pulls you to participate in the world around you—to engage in projects, meet challenges, seize opportunities, and do something with them? What moves you to create, to assert yourself, to be ambitious about yourself? In short, what stirs the fire in your belly?

Is your motivation at the beginning of a project higher than at the end of a project? Do you depend on external sources or internal sources or both to get motivated? Where does your motivation come from, and how do you increase it or ensure that it continues?

Does your motivation vary in its availability and strength? Does it depend on the project, situation, or people involved? Is it a matter of your energy waxing and waning and you need only wait for it to return?

How is your motivation affected by . . .

> . . . the nature of the task or project?

> . . . the goal envisioned?

. . . your physical, emotional, mental
state at the time?

. . . the rewards for getting involved
in the undertaking?

. . . the wish to please someone?

. . . the importance of the activity to you?

. . . the sanctions you will impose
on yourself if you don't engage the
project you've undertaken or the
commitment you've made?

I was so impressed with David, an eighty-seven-year-old economics professor, that I made sure to talk to my son Rob about him. David demonstrated impressive motivation after a serious car accident. A book that he had written got published, and even though he was still recovering, he set about organizing two book-signing parties, adamant that he was going to arrange everything by himself. He later told me, "I anticipated, with fear, that I might not have the energy to do it. I began to fear that I lacked the confidence and that I couldn't do it. But I talked to myself and pushed myself to do it. I did it, and it came off very well."

He explained, "My level of expectation for myself is very high. I talk to myself in the second person and I say, 'I expect you to come across, to produce.' I have to talk to myself all the time, but I don't always listen. Since my accident, I have to push myself to get out of bed, to get washed, to get breakfast, and to do something." He added, "I have a Puritan attitude. Accomplish what you set out to do. Don't stall or put it off. I tell myself, 'You'll make me angry, and in the end you know you're going to do it.'"

David then reflected, "To have an impulse and not be able to do something with it, to have it die, is one of the worst things from a mental health point of view. After a while, you'll stop having an impulse or desire, because you know you're not going to work on it. The impulse will fester and die away and you are left with a lot of unfulfilled desires. These act as a barrier to how you handle impulses in the future. If it becomes a pattern, it could be destructive. I have to keep whipping myself to do it."

When I asked David where he got this life-enhancing motivation, he said, "I guess I really do love life. It's always been exciting to me. I feel that even the small things are lovely. And they keep me in touch with people, and I love people."

TWO

The Emotional Balancing Act

The crucial task of age is balance, a veritable tightrope of balance; keeping just well enough, just brave enough, just gay and interested and starkly honest enough to remain a sentient human being.

> —*The Measure of My Days*
> by Florida Scott-Maxwell

When I was a sophomore in high school, my French teacher assigned an essay on the question "*Quel est le plus bel âge de la vie?*" (What is the most beautiful time of life?) The answer came to me quickly: "Of course: when you are young." Later, in my twenties, I came across a book called *Life Begins at Forty*. I found the title both strange and untrue. I couldn't understand why anyone believed life began at forty when obviously, life was almost over by then. As I look back on these deeply ageist attitudes, I marvel at how I ever came to hold them so firmly and uncritically. I see how unaware I was of the wonderful possibilities of later life, and how much I feared and scorned older age. Today, it's quite clear to me that the best age of my life is the age I am living, creating, and experiencing *now*.

Much of what we always took for granted physically we can no longer assume. Much is harder to do, and the older we get, the harder it is. It's harder to see and hear, harder to walk, breathe, get moving, and keep moving. It's harder to stay awake, to concentrate, to keep warm, to remember what I just did, and to recognize people and know who they are. It's more difficult to fall asleep at night, to sleep deeply, and to get up in the morning. It's not as easy to find my way through once-familiar streets, to deal with complexity, and to stay alert. And it's more trying to put up with nonsense and destructiveness.

By contrast, an Israeli woman of seventy tells me:

> *"I find that everything is becoming 'lighter,' less burdensome, less fateful, as if all the 'vital' decisions—again, for better or for worse—have been taken a long time ago and are a matter of the past.*
>
> *"I also find that with increasing age I experience greater freedom from social pressures,*

especially with regard to my status as a woman who never married or bore children. To me, one of the satisfactions, if not joys, of retirement is that I no longer have to worry about making—or even 'having'—a career. I feel that what I do now is no longer, in any way, part of a 'career.' Having a career in that sense, I feel, is something that, for better or for worse, I have put behind me. What I do now, if I may put it that way, I see as being 'extraterritorial' to any kind of career. I feel that now I no longer have to worry about having myself defined by others according to how I fulfill assignments or demands of any kind. Or about how I am being 'evaluated' or 'assessed' by them in any way. Now it is myself, and no one else, who calls the shots."

Like this woman, I find that some things are also easier for me. It's easier to become impatient, annoyed, frustrated, and critical. It's easier to get tired and drop things. Yet it's also easier to recognize these negative responses and stop some of them. It's easier to be more open-minded, more humane, more understanding, and more empathic. Some things are also clearer: I see myself and my relationships more clearly, and I feel more certain about human nature and the human condition. For example, human beings, with few exceptions, are both good and bad, destructive and constructive, to self and others. They will behave on one or the other side of this duality depending on how they are treated and the social situations they are in.

I've experienced the emotional ups and downs, the contradictions and contrasts, described below. I believe that many of us have had the same experiences.

ENTHUSIASM AND DESPAIR

I've experienced waves of hopelessness and despair, alternating with determination and enthusiasm for living. There have been times—especially when I've been severely ill—when I just wanted to give up and throw in the towel. In those dark moments, I felt that the best days are gone, so why continue at a lesser level of effectiveness? When I see some of the horrendous things that have happened to older people I know, like painful cancer and Alzheimer's, I keep trying to reassure myself that it won't happen to me. After each period of feeling defeated and drained, I return to fight again, to keep on being who I am, who I must be, and to strive for what I might become. Then I become enthusiastic about what I am doing at the moment and what I have yet to do tomorrow, about my current relationships and others that are developing, and about my inner growth and insight.

SECURITY AND INSECURITY

I've experienced increased insecurity because of my increased vulnerability to illness. Uncertainty, over my current illness as well as possible new ones, looms large on my horizon. As time goes on, I will undoubtedly experience some decrease in mental acuity. How long can I continue to be free and independent and pursue projects of my own choosing? How long will I live? In what state? How will my life end? As I think about and experience the reality of these unknowns, I feel anxious and insecure. I therefore have to expect the unpredictable and be ready to meet it in whatever form it takes. But on the other side, I experience myself as being more secure and more integrated. I feel more whole, clearer in my purposes, more certain of my values and the ends that I direct my life toward. I have a wider and broader perspective on life. I feel stronger and surer about what is important and what isn't. My security also comes from feeling stronger about how I cope with adversity. Also, I have established certain routine activities. For example, I see friends and family regularly, exercise routinely, keep my sense of humor engaged, read, write, and teach, as well as meditate regularly and meet with a group that has similar interests to mine. These routines sustain me and provide a degree of equanimity and inner peace much of the time.

FEELING MY AGE AND FEELING AGELESS

I recognize, with a slight shock, that I really don't believe how old I am, and when I do believe it I want to forget it. There are times when I feel every bit of my age: when a strange fatigue hits me, stays a while, and goes away mysteriously; the day after a bad night's sleep, when I try to dance vigorously and find I can keep going for only a few moments. I have to keep reminding myself that I am seventy-six years old. When I remember, I find it difficult to absorb that I have lived so many years. Sometimes, I feel ageless in spirit, as if time had not passed and my young self lingers in the hidden crevices of my being. I am vigorous, walk with a spring in my step, and am full of enthusiasm and energy. I'm often taken aback when someone reflects to me that I present myself to them with an old face, gray hair, and an aged body. To convince myself of my chronological age, I have to keep telling myself: *Be realistic. Much of your life is gone. It's almost over.* How fast and fleeting the past feels! As I approach the end, I want more time—a lot more time. Yet I fear that there may never be enough time. Then I wonder what I should do with my remaining time.

HONESTY AND SELF-DECEPTION

My later years are a time for honesty, especially with myself. (If not now, when?) So I try to confront the truth of my existence, especially the illusions I have about myself and what is happening in and around me. But evading harsh truths about myself or others also has a certain appeal. It's easier not to expose the hypocrisy and deception that prevail in society's social, political, and interpersonal relations. My attempt to be honest with myself *about* myself is a constant struggle.

I must also resist the temptation to avoid looking at my dark side. I think and feel things I'd rather not admit, even to myself. For example, someone disagrees with me and I feel hostile toward him. Someone appears smug and self-satisfied, and I denigrate her to myself. I observe one day, while admiring a younger person's skills, that I also envy him. When I examine my envy, I discover I envy him because he is healthier, more vigorous, stronger than I. Ultimately, I feel he has more

time to live and that my envy is rooted in that difference. Someone I know dies. Mixed with the sadness is
a feeling of gladness that it wasn't me. Or I sometimes
find I am indifferent to another person's illness and
pain, especially if I don't like that person or if I fear that
my own illness is recurring. Or, conversely, I resent another person's good fortune. Or I find myself disliking
someone who is my own age but better off physically
or financially, or more successful socially. I feel guilt or
shame for having such "bad" thoughts. And because of
them, I begin to dislike or think less of myself. Then I
remember that these are only thoughts, only feelings
inside me that I don't have to feel guilty about or act
on, that we all have them. This darker aspect is apt to
escape its cage and crash into our awareness from time
to time, especially when things get more difficult and
we feel that time is running out on us. One way I have
been able to reduce the distressing effects of these unwanted thoughts and feelings is to be fully aware of
them, expect them to occur from time to time, and
see them as outcroppings of my own deprivations and
dissatisfactions, which are inevitable as I grow older.
By recognizing and admitting my dark side to myself
rather than keeping it buried, I can better control how
I express and act on it.

I surely have limitations and self-deceptions that I
am scarcely aware of. I recognize inner states, as well as

behaviors, that I have difficulty confronting, because they are just too painful. Yet I am determined to try to live up to my ideals, to be as authentic as I can, and to be fiercely honest about myself and my relationships. I try to identify the denials, the excuses, and the impulse to take the easier path. In these confrontations with the truth, it is important not to exaggerate, romanticize, or rationalize what I do or who I am. It's also important not to underestimate or devalue myself. Instead, I try to find the reality of whatever is going on, and state it clearly and unequivocally to myself—and, sometimes, to others. But discovering the truth is not a simple matter. There are many sides and layers of truth. There are many complexities, mixtures, and contradictions. There may be only partial truths, not exclusive or universal truths. There may be modified or contaminated truths. But within the context and despite these limitations, I feel the search must continue.

Thus, I ask myself these questions: Who am I really? What have I done? What do I do that is truly good and useful? What do I believe in, and why? How well do I know myself and others? What kinds of relationships do I genuinely have, and what kind do I want? What is important and meaningful to me—important and meaningful enough to make me want to keep on living? What difference has it made that I have lived? What contributions have I made that I'm proud of?

What values do I hold firmly and unequivocally, and why those? What talents do I really have? What potentials have I not yet realized? Should I still try to achieve them? How can I balance my optimism and pessimism? What do I know, and what do I still want to know, about human nature and the human condition? What do I understand about the development and survival of the human race? What does it mean to be fully human, and where am I on that scale?

BEING IN THE WORLD, AND BEING IN ANOTHER WORLD

Being in the world with its concrete demands and being in the spiritual world with its mysteries and unknowns are another pair of contrasting experiences. In the practical, mundane world, I have to make sure that our expenditures don't exceed our income, that I keep my relationships ongoing, that I respond with integrity to those who matter to me, and that I contribute to keeping our household organized and functioning. When I'm in a contemplative mood, the practical issues seem remote to me. At these times, I want to keep a connection to the spiritual domain. For instance, I prefer to read about, talk about, and think about the meaning of life and death and to wonder about the unity of all humankind and the meaning of "the eternal." I look for ways to achieve oneness with nature. I think about those ultimate realities that spiritual writings explore. I would like to experience the exaltation and heightened awareness of the transcendent, which I have only glimpsed during meditation. But the everyday world remains, and my quandary is how to find the holy in the everyday activities and, at the same time, maintain the spiritual as a separate experiential sphere.

SLOW AGING, RAPID AGING

At times, I experience my aging process as a gradual erosion of my physical (and some of my mental) capacities. Each day brings a barely perceptible change. Only in retrospect do I recognize that I am less vigorous, less able to walk up a hill without puffing and needing to rest. At other times, I experience my aging as an abrupt and rapid decline. Only yesterday I had no trouble with my hearing; today I'm having difficulty. Yesterday I scarcely noticed my breathing; today I'm coughing and wheezing and preoccupied with inhaling and exhaling. In each instance, there is a change in self-definition that I must get used to.

I find myself trying to keep up with exactly where I am in the aging process. Catching up and keeping up with my changes as I become a little different! Only in retrospect do I realize that I've moved from one place to another, and that there is a gap between the time I become a little different and the time I recognize it.

EXPERIENCE INTENSIFIED AND EXPERIENCE SUBDUED

Since my illness, I have experienced more deeply my own pain and suffering, as well as the pain of others. I am more empathic with other people's situations and experiences and feel their presence more intensely. At times, I despair about living in dark and deteriorating times. I become angrier and more impatient over greed, arrogance, and egotism.

I also experience greater depth in my own joys and sorrows, and in those of others as well. I laugh more heartily. I am more readily moved to tears by heroic, noble, and poignant actions. I am more affected by classical music and read more voraciously. I recall, as a younger person, how I contained myself when I encountered a beautiful scene—one that was lush and variegated. I somehow couldn't take it all in and allow it to register. Perhaps I feared I would burst with excitement and be overwhelmed by the deliciousness of what I experienced. Or that I would be so inundated with stimuli that I couldn't absorb it all. Now I can let myself feel a scene and let all its beauty seep in slowly. I can let myself experience to the fullest the beautiful, the complex, and the variously new in a more detailed and absorbing way. I am also more involved emotionally with those who care about me. I am more deeply immersed in my relationships and more focused and passionately attached to my projects. I can become more exhilarated by small things. Overall, I feel more alive and vital, more open and vulnerable to the sorrows and delights of living.

On the other hand, there are times when I feel out of it—emotionless, detached, uninterested, and withdrawn. I find it difficult to reach myself and have no desire to reach out to others, nor is it easy for them to reach out to me. I draw into my shell and find a perverse joy in being isolated, feeling sorry for myself, and closing my eyes to the rest of the world. Or I am exhausted, deflated, with no desire to feel anything. I can focus on nothing but my weariness. All I want is rest and recuperation. Recognizing this or having warm contact with a friend usually snaps me out of it.

In another mood, I find myself calm, emotionally uninvolved, looking at myself and others and situations with dispassionate eyes. I feel as if I were on some ledge looking down on the scene, being impartial to all and having no stake or vested interest in what is going on or its outcome. Thus, at various times and places, in various moods, I feel more of everything and less of everything. Both more and less involved, more captured by the moment and more removed from it. I experience these as the alternating strong currents of my aging life.

Learning to come to terms with such opposing pulls is one of the major juggling acts in successful aging. The more skillfully we can balance this swinging between contrasting experiences, the better we age.

THREE

Combining Opposite Orientations

In addition to the emotional balancing act that I experienced and described above, I have noticed that as we grow older, we develop what appear to be opposing or contradictory orientations and ways of being. For example, the wish to be alone is opposed by our desire to carry on relationships; our push to participate in social life is opposed by our pull to withdraw from it. We might be conflicted about which realities we want to face and which ones we wish to avoid or deny. We might work hard to balance the degree of dependence we must accept, with all the ways we can still be independent and self-reliant. Finally, we might have to struggle between letting hope buoy us up and surrendering to despair.

These opposing tendencies might be seen as a clash of opposites or as a struggle in which one side is trying to win out over the other. Or, as I prefer, we can view them not as polarizations or contradictions, but as aspects of the same process—of coming to terms and integrating in later life alternative modes of our becoming and being. I see later life as striving to reconcile these alternatives into a working equilibrium.

ALONENESS AND RELATIONSHIPS

Many of us struggle to strike the right balance between our desire for aloneness and our desire for relationships. If we are dissatisfied when one or the other predominates, we can make the effort to right the balance and, in doing so, find the equilibrium that is "right" for us.

BEING ALONE

Being alone and feeling alone are, at least to some extent, intrinsic parts of being human, and all but inevitable in modern society. As we age and are removed from many of the people and situations that were a part of our life, aloneness becomes even more of an issue.

Others may impose our aloneness on us. Friends and family may have abandoned, avoided, or withdrawn from us because we were too difficult or demanding. Or people close to us may have moved away to a distant city, so that we rarely see them. We may have suffered the death of friends and family and are alone because these intimates cannot be replaced and we have yet to fill the void they left in our lives. Some choose aloneness.

Some of this alone time is rich and fruitful and leaves us feeling buoyant. Some is painful and unwanted and leaves us feeling empty. In the latter case, it behooves us to find ways to come to terms with our aloneness and learn to deal with it positively. This may mean discovering ways to turn unwanted loneliness into serene solitude. And sometimes, it means finding ways to be less alone and more connected to others. Either way, learning to make the most of our alone time empowers us and helps us feel more in control of our lives.

Solitude and loneliness are as different as day and night. The contrast between them is reflected in my account below, on two separate days of aloneness:

This is a day spent musing, reading, reflecting on the book I'm writing, and listening to music. I look forward to meeting a friend in the evening. I review family affairs and make mental notes about the issues I wish to emphasize in the course I am teaching. It is a precious, joyous day, a gentle and quiet day, a luscious day ripe with serenity, a day of sheer delight and pleasure. I have a sense of ease, relaxation, and spaciousness. The day stretches out in an almost unending way as if time is unlimited and enduring. The day has the feel and sense of a week, and I feel I have multiplied the time I have available to be here.

This is an uncomfortable day. I have unpleasant feelings of fatigue in the morning because I did not sleep well. It is difficult to do my exercises, and the tasks I've set for myself require too much energy. I try to meditate and find myself falling asleep. Upon awakening, I'm a little refreshed and try to work on my book, but I feel blocked. I look for some diversion. I read something light, a weekly magazine. I get bored with that. I think of going for a walk or riding my stationary bicycle. I decide I'm too tired for either one. I feel the day dribbling away but surrender to the fact that it is *that* kind of day. Surprisingly, in the evening my energy is renewed as the time comes to meet the friend I will spend the evening with. One of the sustaining things about being alone is the opportunity to look forward to the company of others.

THE SINGULAR JOYS OF SOLITUDE

In contrast to the pain of loneliness, solitude permits satisfying, pleasurable, and instructive experiences that can only be had alone.

Solitude offers the opportunity to thrive on aloneness. It gives us time and leisure to experience ourselves, contemplate our lives, think about the people we associate with, and review our reveries.

Solitude lets us be in a calm, peaceful, quiet environment, doing work we wish to do, thinking through issues we are concerned about, appreciating nature or art, engaging in a spiritual practice. It provides the opportunity to relax and be ourselves, out of other people's control, scrutiny, and judgment. It is a time when we don't have to concern ourselves about performing a role or making an impression. In solitude, we can go to bed and get up when we want, without having to put up with someone else's foibles and idiosyncrasies. In short, solitude permits us to connect deeply with ourselves and our universe.

Solitude also provides the opportunity to explore silence. Ordinarily, our life is full of sound, and silence may be a strange and uncomfortable space between sounds. But getting to know silence as an experience in itself might prove highly instructive.

We usually don't appreciate that silence has its own sound, its own feel, and its own unique impact on us. We can use the silence to discover what is going on inside us, to experience our bodies, examine our subtle feelings, and look at how we fit into that silent space.

Silence can have very different qualities. The "silence of the womb" is pregnant with possibility and heralds the fact that something new is about to be born. Whereas "the silence of the tomb" is heavy: it outlines the inanimate and evokes sadness. Silence is necessary for meditation and, thus, becomes a facilitator of discovering ordinarily inaccessible realms.

I'M LONELY

Unfortunately, not all aloneness is rich with solitude. More often, we are apt to experience loneliness.

It would be remarkable if any of us never felt lonely. In fact, some Native American wisdom holds that the only thing that all humans have in common is our loneliness. We undoubtedly have all suffered loneliness at different times throughout our lives.

As we all know, loneliness is an inner ache when we are not aware of being connected to ourselves, others, nature, or anything else. We can certainly feel lonely in a crowd or in a relationship. But by and large, most of us feel loneliest when we are physically alone. Loneliness can vary in quality, duration, and intensity from a penetrating pain that aches for a human touch or voice, to a scarcely recognized sense of something being absent. It also might include a sense of isolation, humiliation, emptiness, abandonment, and a feeling of distance from human contact. We may feel that no one is interested

in us or even cares about us. These discomforts of loneliness may be short-lived or long-term.

If you wish to make your loneliness more than an
uneasy compromise with life, here are some ways that
might alleviate your loneliness.

EXAMINE YOUR ALONENESS

Often, loneliness is so painful and scary that we can't
bear to look it in the eye. Yet objectively observing it
can give us profound insights that help diminish our
loneliness. If you want to shed light on the sources of
your isolation and suffering, ask yourself: Am I all alone
because I distrust others or feel insecure about their
intentions? Or is it because I have low self-esteem and
fear that others will discover my flaws and not find me
interesting or worthwhile? Does my loneliness stem
from past difficulty in relationships, which I fear repeat-
ing in the present? Is it because I have been betrayed,
injured, rejected, disappointed, or angered by others?
Or have I withdrawn from others because I've been resented and envied before and don't want those feelings
directed at me again?

Perhaps I have felt contempt and disrespect from
others and it makes me want to disengage from relationships.

Any of the above situations may be contributing

to our loneliness, but they needn't be permanent conditions. If we choose to, we can begin to find ways of changing the causes of our loneliness even if we're not convinced it's worth it. Sometimes, a little reaching out goes a long way.

STRETCH YOUR IMAGINATION

Another way to deal with your loneliness is to stretch your imagination by using books, movies, or TV to ask yourself, for example, what the world was like twenty thousand years ago and what it will be like a thousand years from now. What will human beings be like in five hundred years? Try to imagine what is socially possible in the near and distant future. Develop your image of a supreme being or of the power in the universe or explore what it means to attain spiritual enlightenment. On a smaller scale, imagine the ideal way to furnish and decorate your home. Or fantasize about how it would feel to radically change your wardrobe, and what life would be like if you were to do so. You can also work at improving your recall with memory exercises, get regular physical exercise, try meditation as a way of quieting and calming yourself as well as getting in touch with the spiritual domain. Experience your physical environment—how you move in it and the impact it has on you.

AWAKEN YOUR SENSES

Even if you've done everything you can do to change your situation, there may still be times when you find yourself feeling lonely. When loneliness gets you down, sometimes the best solution is simply trying to take your mind away from it. During these times, exploring the sensual side of life can be surprisingly comforting.

There are a thousand things you can do to take your mind off your sorrow and redirect it into other channels and carefully examine a variety of experiences that register through your senses. Pay close attention to the sights, sounds, tastes, and smells that enter your awareness. For example, find delight in your sense of touch by exploring the surfaces in your room and the materials that cover your furniture. Feel the smoothness of silk, the roughness of unpolished wood, the plush surface of a rug. Experience the unusual sensation of the edges of a leaf. Explore the flavors in food: sweet, sour, savory, sharp; in liquids, the subtle taste of water and the variety of tastes in juices and liqueurs. You might luxuriate in the sound of a moving symphony, the hushed rustle of long grass in the breeze, the vitality of street noises. You can pay attention to sounds that are soothing, like gentle rain on the roof, or the twittering of a goldfinch.

Look carefully at what you can see within the

confines of your living space: the shapes, color, density, height, and arrangement of objects; the intersection and meeting of different things, colors, materials; the aesthetic and functional nature of the various pieces of furniture in your room; the brightness of late-afternoon sun on the wall.

Look closely at your hand and see the minutest of its details: the texture, the color of the skin, its wrinkles, the shape of your fingers, the color of your fingernails, how the knuckles bend and your fingers extend. Look at the palm of your hand and its lines and crevices, each finger and how it moves with the others, the size of your fist, the strength in your arm. Smell your skin. Feel its smoothness or roughness, how your hand fits together as a whole and how it relates to the whole of the other hand.

Looking outside, can you see a lovely sunrise or sunset, the houses, trees, and sky, all in interesting configurations, colors, and intensities?

Explore your kinesthetic sense. Nonjudgmentally notice the feel of your body, how you carry its weight, how you walk, and how you sit, the pains and pleasures, the stance you take as you occupy space.

Detect the different scents in different rooms of your home, and compare them with the scents outdoors. Outside, it smells like evergreens and wet grass. In the kitchen, there might be a coffee smell or an odor of beginning-to-spoil food; in the living room, there might be a gentle but faintly discernible fragrance of a vase of lilies. Go to a nearby garden or woodland and feast your senses on the ever-renewing world of nature. Go wine tasting. Enjoy the flavors and aromas of exotic foods.

By concentrating on things, events, and situations outside yourself, you might alleviate some of your feelings of loneliness.

Ultimately, to fight loneliness we must try to identify its sources and look for correctives. We can often make something positive out of it by converting it to solitude or transforming it into a less painful state. Love, and being with those we love, is often the best cure. Creative projects in which we lose ourselves and deeply invest our attention and energy can be like an elixir. Finally, we can work at enduring, accepting, or transcending our feelings of loneliness—managing them so they don't interfere with our functioning or drag us down. The mere fact that we've made it to later life means that we have done a lot of living. Hence, we are some of the most fascinating people around, with much inner wealth to share with others and the world, if we'll only let it out.

While loneliness may be part of the human condition, there are ways to soften its blows. We can invite or seek a new relationship or push forward one that is just starting, or seek out someone we are currently associated with, and turn an acquaintance into a friend.

I AND THOU (AND OTHERS): RELATIONSHIPS

In later life, how alone we are and the number of relationships we have may be more important than before. In the swirl of family building and working life, we are necessarily pulled into relationships. We may want to be alone more than before or to be selective about who we associate with. On the other hand, we might find ourselves alone more than we like, and recognize that we are having trouble finding the kinds of relationships we want.

For most of us in later life, relationships make for a more satisfying existence. We need someone to talk with and share our thoughts, pains, and joys. We need to experience the reality of the other as a live human being interacting with us and thus affirming our own existence. We value our relationships because through them we are cherished, valued, and validated. They afford us the opportunity to make deep connections with others, out of which we can invent and invigorate our later lives.

Relationships take many different forms: long-term

or short-term, casual or intense, superficial or intimate, intermittent or continuous. They may be meaningful or relatively insignificant, weak or strong, troublesome or harmonious, recent or tried-and-true.

The reasons and bases for a relationship also vary. They can arise from a mutual and reciprocal emotional commitment, grounded in love for each other. A relationship can also arise from hating and fighting with each other. They can be based on mutual benefit or habit and routine. They can stem from one or both partners' fear of leaving the relationship because they fear loneliness or fear being seen as undesirable. One partner may be dominant, with one or both liking it that way and staying together for that reason. They can be a product of mutual interests or common goals, or they may result from separate interests attainable through the relationship. And they can stem from need, dependency, or interdependency.

For some older people, maintaining an intimate relationship with someone we care about is enough to make life worthwhile. For others, intimate relations are necessary but not sufficient for a satisfying life. We need something more: working at a project, creating a spiritual pursuit, joining a group or organization, studying or developing knowledge in an area of interest. For many, the bane of our existence is that we do not have close, intimate relationships, and this puts a negative cast on our entire lives. Or, conversely, we may desire fewer and less intimate relationships.

If our intimates of early life are gone, it may not be easy to develop new friendships. Both the person we are trying to form a relationship with and we ourselves may be shy and awkward, hesitant to open up and reveal our inner selves. Yet without relationships, we can feel adrift and disconnected.

Most of us would like to stay positively connected: loving and caring for each other, pursuing shared lives. Unfortunately, at times we are pulled apart: out of fear; by not understanding each other; because of competitiveness, dislike, or disrespect; or because we have different expectations, values, and personalities.

Despite the problems and difficulties in relationships, most of us in later age would like to have an intimate relationship or a friendship, same sex or opposite sex, in which there is caring, tenderness, concern, respect, appreciation, trust, and meaningfulness. We all long for love, affectionate bonding, and deep positive feelings in our intimate connections and attachments. We want our partners to be as concerned about our welfare as they are about their own, and vice versa. To most of us, being cared for and being cared about in later life is one of our central concerns. The need to be cared for and cared about gets stronger, not weaker, as we move into the later years. Most importantly, intimate relationships are a source of physical exchange and tenderness that enhance our self-esteem and are vitally sustaining for our emotional and physical well-being. As doubts grow about our desirability and attractiveness, we need reassurance. Ideally, this comes from our spouse, siblings, neighbors, children or grandchildren, and friends who still care about us and want to be with us.

We usually seek one or more of these in an intimate relationship: companionship, warmth, physical and sexual relations, honest exchanges, or sharing our deepest feelings and thoughts. It includes being sensitive to each other's needs and being ready to fulfill them. Hopefully, we are spontaneous with each other, giving each other comfort, support, reassurance, and mutual respect and being as concerned about the other's well-being as we are about our own.

Awareness of the nature of our relationships and aloneness might enable us to discover the various paths and people with whom we can and wish to share our pursuits at this stage of our life.

PROBLEMS AND ISSUES IN RELATIONSHIPS

It would be most unusual if a relationship were not attended by some problems and difficulties. Here are some issues we often confront in making new relationships or maintaining old ones.

Having lost—either by departure or through death—a dear friend or an intimate relative with whom we had a caring, close relationship, we may now feel she or he cannot be replaced, and so we are unwilling even to try to find someone who might be like them or might begin to fill the void they left in our lives.

Over time, we may have had disrupted, broken, and abandoned relationships. We may have rejected people we used to be friendly with, or vice versa. We may be estranged from a son or a daughter. A long relationship may wear out to the point that there is not much meaning or interest in it, for us or the other, and we've drifted apart. Maybe we abandoned a relationship because there was too much conflict and hostility and too many bitter, angry exchanges.

In reviewing these abandoned relationships, we can ask ourselves if we want to do anything about repairing or restarting any of them. If so, can we identify those that have some possibilities for rehabilitation? Is there still too much pain, disappointment, resentment, or distrust? Or have these feelings subsided enough for us to take some baby steps toward rebuilding them?

If the right kinds of relationships aren't there, we may feel it acutely. Perhaps, we are not sure how to go about it, and who we wish to connect with. We might feel insecure about whether we can indeed make or maintain a relationship. How do we identify the people we might be interested in, and how do we seek them out and make contact? Would it help us to make our wish explicit to a third party who might be able to facilitate things? *Is* there someone who could help make it happen?

We may lack sufficient motivation to form relationships, even though a part of us would like to. Shyness, fear of rejection, previous failures, and low self-esteem might stand in our way, so we believe that others will not be interested in us. We might think we need a lot of energy to form a relationship, and feel that our energy level is too low. Whatever stands in our way, we can struggle to overcome it.

Maybe, we don't know whether we even want any relationship. Or we try to make relationships, but we don't succeed. We are rejected by people we want a relationship with, and rebuff those who reach out to us, and we don't quite understand why it isn't working out.

Perhaps, the relationships we have are not satisfying because we and the other are temperamentally unsuited for each other or because we find the other dull. Or maybe the relationship is too superficial—has too little depth of feeling or understanding to be meaningful to us.

Sometimes, there are too many conflicts and misunderstandings, too much scapegoating, blaming, and unresolved bitterness between us and the other. Our self-esteem is too often attacked or eroded in the relationship. We are too demanding, or the other person expects too much of us. Either way, there is not enough love, caring, warmth, and commitment. Thus, we don't get what we need and want.

It may be that we don't have enough freedom in the relationship and thus feel constrained, or that we can't rely on the other person when we need them. Maybe the relationship has been built on too much insincerity and hypocrisy. Or, for some unknown reason, the relationship evokes fear or discomfort in us.

Sometimes, the relationship is not one we have freely chosen. It has been forced or imposed on us, or we feel an obligation to maintain it. And now we want out and don't know quite how to do it.

If a relationship has been going on for a long time, it can "go on autopilot," proceeding now on the basis of habit and routine. There isn't much pleasure or enthusiasm in it for us, yet we are uncertain whether we want to end it. We may need the relationship because we are dependent on the other, and yet we are uncomfortable with that dependency. Even though we may feel merely tolerated by the other, when we contemplate the loss of this relationship, we're apprehensive about it. We feel that we'll be losing something valuable that the other has to offer, or that we'll be deprived if we give up the relationship.

Relationships can have many unresolved issues. We may not even know exactly what they are, yet we feel the lack of resolution. Or we know what the issues are, but we can't talk about them because the other will get defensive or wouldn't understand. Maybe we have identified the issues and raised them, but they haven't been successfully resolved.

Our wish for privacy and some of our own idiosyncrasies can make it difficult putting up with the presence of others. This restricts the kind of relationships that we can have. On the other hand, we can have *too* many relationships and see too many people, too often, and end up feeling that we don't have enough time to relax and be at ease with ourselves.

We can reflect on these things and identify those relationship issues that are current for us, and ask ourselves what, if anything, we would like to do about them. We can find the best way to come to terms with them—let them be, confront them, ignore them, deny them, engage them, try to transcend them, or explore ways of overcoming them.

PARTICIPATION AND WITHDRAWAL

Whether we participate in the social world or withdraw from it is related, in part, to the kind of relationships we have or want to have. In part, it depends on how motivated we are to be active in the world of social affairs.

In later life, we experience opposing tendencies. On the one hand, we feel the impulse to withdraw into privacy and our own cocoon, to disengage from social activities and become more reclusive, isolated, and self-involved. On the other hand, many of us are pulled into greater participation in group, community, or political activities. With more free time, we can engage the social world that we simply didn't have time for when our lives were busier. Different people feel pulled this way or that, and we may have these opposing impulses and drives pulling us in opposite directions.

Do you experience tension between reducing and increasing your social participation? Between withdrawing from and engaging in projects with other people? Does a certain degree of weariness or disinterest create an attitude of "Why bother?" or "I don't care to be involved"? Or are you primed and eager to "get in there," to embrace new activities and enterprises, and especially to participate in building a caring community? Are you enthusiastic about social, political, economic, or recreational activities? What is the balance in your life between disengaging and withdrawing from activities, and being involved and interested in the world at large? You might be torn between pursuing group activities or participating in social causes or projects that contribute to the welfare of others, and remaining detached, aloof, and resistant to participation. Doing things with a group draws on your life energy, your motivation, your curiosity, and your desire to be connected with, and contribute to, collective life. Conversely, the wish to remain detached and aloof might derive from your passivity, your diminished energy, and your indifference to the ongoing social process. The tension as I've experienced it is between, on the one hand, being passive and not doing anything with others, having no desire to exert myself, but rather seeking comfort and relaxation; and, on the other hand, being preoccupied and not wanting to be obligated to others for my time and energy. This is opposed by my getting up in the morning with enthusiasm and eagerness to pursue the projects I've chosen to participate in and to join with others in a collective effort of importance, to them and to me.

Many of us have the opportunity to make a conscious choice between being connected with, and being separated from, others in a group enterprise. We can choose between belonging and not belonging to groups—doing little or nothing of social usefulness, versus making some contribution to the group, community, or society.

What are some of the reasons you might move in one or the other direction? You might withdraw because you want the relaxation and don't want the discomfort that comes from active participation and involvement with others in a group's activities. You might feel that the world is a dangerous place and you don't want to expose yourself to it. You might withdraw because of bitterness and resentment against a world that has denied you, injured you grievously, or caused you much pain and suffering. You might feel a sense of futility about your actions because you have, in some way, given up and surrendered to despair. Or you believe that whatever you might do would be of little use, unimportant and meaningless to anyone else. You might be so preoccupied with your own difficulties that you haven't the time, energy, or interest to get involved in more people's problems in a common cause or enterprise.

On the other hand, you may want to participate with others out of altruism—because you are eager to be helpful to others as a way of keeping yourself energized, engaged, and involved with life. Or it could be out of concern for the well-being of others and the survival of the planet. Or maybe you just want to maintain deep connections with your social world while developing a caring community. Are you driven by a fierce determination to carry on projects with others, or are you burdened with surrender and passivity?

If you've decided to try to increase your participation in the social world, here are some ideas to help you determine the directions you might take and the ways you might make a contribution to others.

You might join a group that discusses something from the news of the day, or a weekly prayer group. Or maybe you feel a growing concern over climate change and the continuing degradation of our environment. If so, check out environmental protection groups working to stop pollution and the destruction of our natural resources.

There is so much social, political, and economic dysfunction and abuse in our society that you can easily find a way to pitch in. For example, you might find it gratifying to be an adopted grandparent for a child who has none, or a tutor for an underprivileged child. You can join a group that opposes nuclear testing, or join a political club to work for a candidate or party you would like to see elected.

The local community might be able to use your services. Could you be a safety officer at a street crossing for elementary school children? A docent at a local museum? Or a volunteer at a community hospital? Work with a rehabilitation program for young people with problems? Serve as a volunteer to answer the phone on a hotline for emotionally disturbed persons? Teach in an after-school crafts program? Community centers have many programs and group activities for senior citizens that might benefit you physically, emotionally, and socially if you joined them. And if it doesn't exist in your neighborhood, what will it take to get one started?

Become a member of a collectivity pursuing a common goal that has humanitarian purposes. You may well have your own humanity reinforced, and you'll have the opportunity to confirm the humanity of others. Thus, you'd feel yourself a member of a human community in a way that you may not have felt before.

FACING REALITY—OR NOT

There may be times and situations when we are undecided whether to face a particular reality or avoid it—stare it in the face and come to terms with it, or ignore it.

Is your general disposition to confront or not to confront reality? Of the multiple realities we are asked or forced to face, any particular one can present a challenge in how much, or even whether, we want to face it. Thus, knowing ourselves, our predispositions, and the conditions under which we avoid or face a reality may help us deal with a particularly puzzling or difficult one.

There are many realities we have to confront and deal with every day to function in the world. There also are many realities we avoid, deny, flee from, or ignore every day—because they are unpleasant, harmful, or simply too difficult to bear. If we don't have to pay too steep a price for such avoidance, we probably will go right on avoiding that reality.

UNDERSTANDING THE NATURE OF A REALITY

Before you can face a reality, you have to know what it is. Sometimes, it's quite obvious or easy to discover. If the reality is clouded or uncertain—such as whether you actually have lost some mental acuity—the first task is to observe, test, then evaluate as best you can what is so, until you come to some tentative conclusion about what the reality is and how it is affecting you.

Admitting an important new event into our consciousness may be only the first step in what may turn out to be a complex process of facing reality. This process involves a number of questions: Is it an immediate and urgent reality (for example, a broken leg), or is it one that doesn't require immediate action (say, a slight cough or sniffle)?

Is it a temporary condition (such as a hangnail, a cold, a burned wrist), or a more or less permanent one (such as chronic illness)? That is, will it go away, or is it here to stay?

Is it fixed and constant, or changing? It can be constant, like a short-term memory loss, or changing and not necessarily for the better, such as gradual loss of energy over time. Thus, we need to ask: What is it now, compared with what it will be in the future? It may be difficult to know whether it's fixed or changing. For example, after an automobile accident, you may have severe headaches, but you don't know if they will remain with you the rest of your life.

Some realities are not clear and are open to different interpretations. For example, if your friend has a nasty temper and often shows it to you, it's a clear-cut reality. On the other hand, if your friend is unusually inactive, the reality of what is going on with him may be ambiguous or obscure. Some people may think he's depressed; others may think he's just taking it easy after a rough patch; still others may think he's in his meditative mood. Often, there are different interpretations of the same reality and of what, if anything, needs to be done about it.

Is the reality something completely new (e.g., instability and imbalance when walking)? Or is it something you've had before that has disappeared and has come back and therefore is familiar to you (for example, dizzy spells)? Is it threatening to your basic health and security (for example, failing eyesight or hearing loss), or is it benign?

Does this reality appear in a mild or a severe form? Can something be done about it (for example, a boil on your arm)? Or is it impossible to do anything about it (for example, failing eyesight due to macular degeneration)? If something can be done about it, do you want to try, or does someone else have to do something about it, either at your request or on their own initiative? Or do you want to postpone acting on it until sometime in the future?

Realities arrive by various routes. It can be imposed on you by accident (e.g., a wrenched shoulder in a fall). It can arise from life processes (e.g., your aging causes greater difficulty in hearing and seeing). You can create it by an unwitting action (for example, your hostility disrupts a relationship). You can inadvertently choose it (you walk into a dangerous neighborhood and are attacked and injured), or you can choose it deliberately (for instance, a difficult course in mathematics). It can happen in the course of living, when a loved one becomes severely ill. A reality, whether chosen, imposed, or the product of an accident, forces us into a decision about the stance we will take toward it, and what we may do about it.

DECIDING WHETHER TO FACE A REALITY

In some instances, avoiding a reality is not a conscious choice. It happens outside your awareness, and you unconsciously dismiss it until something intervenes. In other instances, you may make a deliberate or semi-conscious decision to avoid a reality. In these instances, there are a number of considerations to take into account in determining whether to face a particular reality.

The particular kind of reality it is, and how it arose, may make certain ones easier to face than others. The reality can be so overwhelming, persistent, and intrusive that you must recognize it (though you still may or may not *do* anything about it)! The degree to which the reality stirs up strong emotions such as fear for your welfare or survival, or overwhelming despair, will influence your decision, as will the severity of the pain or suffering the reality is causing you.

How much control will you lose over your life, for how long, if you choose to face and act on the reality? How about if you choose to avoid it? How easy or difficult is it emotionally to face this reality, versus to avoid it. You may feel that you will be better able to face this particular reality in the future because some of the other realities that are currently impinging on you and requiring more immediate attention will be gone by then.

What actions must you take to face this reality? What is the degree of unpleasantness or distress associated with these actions? Do you lean toward facing certain realities, such as physical dysfunctions, because they may limit you in unacceptable ways if you don't face them? Are the people who might support you in facing a particular reality available and ready to step up?

How frequently—continually, or only at a particular time—must you face a particular reality? What are the consequences for each option? Is your action or inaction in your best interest? In other words, what physical, emotional, economic, or social price will you pay for facing it now versus facing it later? Is this the best situation and the best place to face it? Is this the time to face it? Which stance toward this reality gives you the most comfort and peace of mind?

Here are some important realities in later life you may have to consider: You can face or avoid the reality of who you are. If you opt for confrontation, honesty, and insight about yourself, you may discover that you're better than you thought! Maybe you're kinder and more concerned for others. But you may also discover that you are worse than you thought you were. Maybe you are more self-indulgent, more hostile or indifferent to others, more unpleasant.

You can choose to face or avoid the reality of your relationships, especially the important ones. By facing the true state of a particular relationship, you may be surprised or disappointed. But regardless of the pain or joy involved, you will at least know where you stand.

You can confront, avoid, or deny the reality of your aging. With awareness, you have an opportunity to make the physical and emotional adjustments necessary for your changing condition. But such a confrontation can bring up worry, fear, and a sense of helplessness. On the other hand, denial or avoidance may stave off continuing concern or anxiety, at least for a little while, and sometimes for much longer.

You can face or avoid the reality of an illness or disability. In the former case, you recognize and accept your illness or disability, and you may try to do something about it. You also can develop an attitude and an emotional adjustment that might enable you to prevent the disability from dominating your life. Delaying recognition or denying your illness might make you put off taking necessary measures to deal with it, until it is too late.

Facing the reality of our own death can bring up preoccupation, fear, acceptance, or preparation for it without too much concern and discomfort—or all these at different times. Denial can come in various forms: unconsciously believing that you are immortal and that it won't happen to you; thinking it is a long way off and need not concern you now.

WAYS OF FACING REALITY

Facing a reality involves bringing it into focal awareness, recognizing it for what it is, letting it enter your consciousness fully and deeply, and responding to it in some way. Thus, you might engage it, grapple with it, deal with it in your own way, and finally do whatever you can about it.

In describing different ways of facing or avoiding reality, it's important to remember, there are varying degrees of doing so. You can face a particular reality fully, jumping in with both feet, or you can face another one as little as possible or not at all. And you may face yet another off and on, depending on your mood and energy level.

In general, your choice to face a reality depends on the nature of the reality and its immediate and potential consequences for your life. You can confront it head-on and try to do something about it (e.g., seeing a doctor for an aching ear that feels infected). Or you can try to come to terms with a reality that is not changeable (e.g., damage has been done to the ear; you have hearing loss and get a hearing aid).

You might approach a reality slowly and gradually, absorbing it bit by bit. For example, let's say a dear friend has been diagnosed with cancer and is given six months to live. At first, you can't believe it—he looks and acts so vital and alive. Then the initial shock wears off and you gradually absorb the idea of his impending death as he gets weaker and weaker and grows more pallid.

You can look with defiance at a reality and try to

stare it down. As in "I don't give a damn that I have pneumonia; I'm going out anyway." You might accept another reality for what it is: genuinely believing, experiencing, absorbing, and assimilating the previously denied, absent, or rejected happening as inescapably present, and act on it or not. For example, you finally come to accept your spouse's departure from your home.

My asthma is a part of me, and I have to live with that. You accept a reality as part of your being.

AVOIDING REALITY

T. S. Eliot observed, "Human kind cannot bear very much reality." One might therefore suppose that denying and avoiding reality is frequent and not all bad. Sometimes, it goes a long way in keeping us going and restraining our fears. But sometimes, denial or avoidance is injurious because a condition or situation might worsen while we steadily refuse to recognize it. The issue is to figure out what degree of avoidance or denial, under what circumstances, is functional, appropriate, and not too risky. Sometimes, distorting, avoiding, or denying reality serves our purpose. It maintains our self-esteem, proves us right in our own minds, and helps us see ourselves in a favorable light, in a situation more like we wish it to be. Positive illusions may provide hope for the future, sustain a mood of positive expectations, and let you carry on. The issue is how long and how well we can maintain that hope. We can't predict when the illusion will be destroyed. If that happens, hope can turn into despair or a disturbed flight from reality. I am here reminded of the Eugene O'Neill play *The Iceman Cometh*, in which the hero, after having stayed many years in a barroom, finally goes out to face the outside world. He quickly discovers that he cannot face reality "out there," so he returns to the barroom to live indefinitely with his illusions. O'Neill's point here is that without our illusions, without the capacity to avoid certain realities, we might indeed be unable to survive.

For many of us, our first impulse is to avoid or ignore a most unpleasant reality. There are several ways to do it, as well as different degrees of avoidance. This can vary from a quick glimpse to a complete repression. You can deliberately and self-consciously refuse to accept it. For example, before I went on a trip to China, I had been diagnosed with chronic bronchitis. I was told that Chinese cities were badly polluted and that I risked making the illness worse if I visited there. I chose to ignore that warning, took the trip, and came down with asthma.

Or you might unconsciously and unwittingly repress the reality. For example, when you are completely oblivious to your failing eyesight and someone calls it to your attention, you deny it outright. Or you might put off facing reality—for example, by refusing to see a physician after you've had ongoing pain in your stomach for many months. Or you can vaguely and occasionally recognize that your hearing is failing, but most of the time, you forget about it, ignore it, or act as if it were not so. Or you can be so frightened when you face a particular reality, or when you have it pushed in your face, that you flee from it and refuse to accept it as real— for example, a positive HIV test result. Or you might refuse to recognize the loss of a talent or skill you once had, as when a ballet dancer or opera singer finds they can't perform as well as before, yet they persist in performing, to unwelcome results.

The process of avoidance might come about by your refusal to let the reality exist at all in your experience. You might recognize it and dismiss it as being of no consequence, or you might recognize it and put off paying any real attention to it until a later time. Or you can delude yourself into thinking that the reality is something else, or develop some illusion about it, which diminishes or eliminates its severity and importance to you.

Some of us combine facing reality and avoiding it, in an alternating fashion. We jump from one to the other until we settle on one or the other. Or it may be more of a continuous vacillation. This may very well be the case in confronting the reality of our eventual death, and the fear associated with it.

The issue, then, is to find the optimal balance between facing a reality and avoiding it. For any particular reality, we must determine whether, how, when, where, and with whom to face or avoid it. The tension is between facing reality, thereby knowing what it is, understanding it, and doing something about it if that is possible and necessary. And if doing something about it is *not* possible and necessary, at least you know where you stand in relation to what is real. And in avoiding the reality that can't be (or doesn't need to be) fixed, you are—perhaps temporarily, perhaps indefinitely—diminishing the fear, difficulty, and confusion associated with it. You are making the conscious decision to risk incurring negative future consequences in order to function more effectively and comfortably in the present.

DEPENDENCY AND SELF-RELIANCE

Most of us in later life want to keep control of our lives, being as much in charge as we were in younger years. We want to take as much responsibility for ourselves as we can: make our own decisions, be autonomous, carry out our own plans, move physically by ourselves, stay alert, and challenge ourselves to be active. We want to do the things we need and would like to do, stay connected with others we have chosen, and be constructively occupied on projects we wish to pursue. We want to be independent, in control, and self-reliant as well as interdependent and self-directed.

You may rage at your dependency, surrender to it in despair, or accept it with equanimity. But increasing dependency and the need for help is inevitable as we grow older. It may be only a little, or we may need more help from specific people for certain things at certain times. Or we may face a more generalized, pervasive dependency much or all of the time. One issue that can arise in this blending of dependency and self-reliance is how to acknowledge the inevitability of our being dependent in at least some areas of our life, and then be able to accept this by getting and keeping the help we need. The question is whether you can evaluate your capabilities, neither over- nor underestimating them.

The tension may be between exaggerating how self-reliant you can be, perhaps straining or injuring yourself in the process, and being overly dependent, avoiding stretching yourself whenever you can. The challenge for each of us is to be dependent when we ought to be, and know how much and what kind of help to seek when the nature of our functioning indicates that we should. This requires knowing both yourself and the nature of the tasks you are undertaking. Thus, the challenge is to find a realistic and appropriate balance between dependency and self-reliance that fits our condition and our capabilities. And we must walk the fine line between overdependency and rash self-reliance. Also, we must appraise and readjust that balance over time as our physical, emotional, and external circumstances change. A major difficulty in doing this arises when we are uncertain about our abilities and capabilities, about what kind, and how much, help we need and from whom. Who's to judge this besides us ourselves? Can you trust your own judgment, and can you rely on someone else to help you make this judgment?

I have found that there is often a tension, based on our emotional state, between the obvious need of help from someone for something, and resistance to accepting that help or even admitting the need for it. There may be a parallel tension between our emotional predisposition to believe we are less capable of performing a task, and the reality of our capabilities, which, if tested, would reveal that we can do so much more than we thought we could. In the former case, we are dealing with exaggerated independence and self-reliance; and in the latter case, with exaggerated dependency and need for help.

THE PRICE OF STUBBORNNESS

I recall my strong resistance to taking steroids. When I developed asthma, my pulmonologist urged me to take steroids in addition to other medications to control my asthma. But a psychologist who himself had asthma and treated persons with the illness using behavioral therapy strongly advised me not to take steroids, because of their addictive quality. He believed—and had much evidence to show—that once you begin steroids and continue on them for some time, you never get off them. In the long run, depending on the daily dosage and number of years you have taken them, steroids might have serious negative effects on various internal organs. Using the psychologist's advice to validate my own resistance, I refused to take the steroids for the first nine months after I developed asthma, and I suffered greatly as a consequence. During those nine months, I had several asthmatic attacks and was admitted to the emergency room twice and hospitalized twice. I kept struggling with the decision. At age sixty-seven, this was the first time in my life that I had to decide whether I would take the first step toward becoming dependent on medication for the rest of my life. At the end of nine months, it became obvious that I could not continue to refuse steroids if I wanted to live in any acceptable way—or live at all, since the attacks were becoming more serious and more frequent. Finally, at my doctor's insistence, I agreed to try five milligrams of prednisone. The medication had a profound effect in altering the course of my illness. With it, I could almost be normal again. As a consequence, I surrendered to steroid dependency and expected—not with eagerness or happiness, but at least with some relief—to be dependent on steroids into the indefinite future.

ACCEPTING HELP GRACEFULLY

There are times when temporary dependency is appropriate.

I was returning from a vacation with two heavy suitcases that were at the airport baggage claim. In addition, I was carrying a few light pieces of luggage off the plane. My airplane companion during the flight, a middle-aged man with whom I had a very pleasant conversation, offered to retrieve my bags from the carousel and carry them to a cabstand for me. My first thought was, *I can handle them. I really don't need his help. He undoubtedly thinks of me as a weak, asthmatic old man with a bad back.* Both these physical limitations had come up in our conversation. A second thought quickly followed: *It will be something of a struggle to manage all this luggage myself, and he really wants to be helpful. I'll let him help me with his greater physical strength.* I let him carry my luggage and thanked him heartily, and he seemed very pleased at my gratitude.

Even when there are good reasons for accepting help, we should expect certain emotional difficulties that come with being less self-reliant and more dependent. First, we feel the increased sense of powerlessness and loss of control, often followed by a loss of self-esteem, and a feeling of inadequacy as a person. If you have been an independent and self-directed person, it isn't easy to give up that control (or have it taken out of your hands). It's hard to deliver yourself into the hands of a caretaker, authority, or expert, or to be taken over by a physical agent such as a medication, especially if you have valued independence throughout your life. Your inner protest might ring loud and clear through various manifestations of denial, resistance, and refusal before you finally surrender. It may take time to absorb and come to terms with your dependency. In the meantime, you might be besieged by fantasies of helplessness, or fears of becoming a vegetable or getting dementia. Restrictions on your independence and control over your life may bring up frustration and anger and impel you to fight your dependency in various ways, both reasonable and unreasonable. You may try to hide or minimize your dependency. The haunting issue is how much dependency, and of what kinds, will induce despair. Does your dependency make you feel ashamed, embarrassed, hopeless, or stigmatized?

How you feel about your dependency will depend in part on those you rely on for help: how sympathetic and empathic they are, how well they understand your needs, how much they encourage you to be self-reliant and independent in areas where you can be. Do they take a condescending or pitying attitude toward you, or do they let you be of help to them in areas where you have greater competence or information? Do they continue to respect you and communicate to you that your dependency is only a part of your "self" and that you are much more than that?

Janet Belsky, in her book *Here Tomorrow*, quotes a study that shows how demoralizing being on the receiving end can be. It found that people who got help from family "tried to reciprocate in some way [*and*] when they could not balance the getting with at least some giving, they tended to be depressed . . . So if you have to accept help, try to give something in return. Explain that you need to reciprocate for your own self-esteem."[4]

Some of us never admit our need to be dependent. Others are ready to accept dependency whenever they can. Still others approach dependency in a matter-of-fact way, without a lot of drama. Perhaps, you can learn to be dependent in a way that is not injurious to your self-esteem and represents that elusive balance we discussed: to ask for help when you really need it, use help when it seems a reasonable thing to do, reject help when

---

4 Janet Belsky, *Here Tomorrow* (Baltimore: Johns Hopkins University Press, 1988), 132.

you don't need it, and feel secure about managing by yourself when your own powers are equal to the occasion.

My friend David's strong need to be self-reliant showed up when he started to make progress getting around after an accident. As soon as he got into the wheelchair, he didn't want anyone to push it. He insisted on spinning the wheels himself. When he could get up from the wheelchair, he didn't want anyone to help him. He would pull himself up. When he began to walk with a cane, he didn't want anyone to hold his elbow. He insisted on getting in and out of a car by himself. When driven to a pathway adjacent to an apartment that he was going to enter, he again manifested his independence. The pathway was some fifty feet long and had a slight upward incline. He nevertheless pushed himself to walk all the way, aided only by his cane and rejecting any and all help. He said, "I want to do as much as I can by myself." And then he did.

HOPE AND DESPAIR

A famous poem states, "Hope springs eternal," but it says nothing about hopelessness and despair, which are also recurrent emotions, especially in later life.[5] To lead

---

5 Alexander Pope, *An Essay on Man*, Epistle I, 95.

a joyous, fulfilling life, we must develop a balance that favors hope over despair, and find ways of easing or reducing despair so that hope predominates.

It is a rare person who hasn't, at various times in life, experienced both hope and despair. As we grow older, the tension between these two opposites may become stronger, and the need to reconcile and bring them into some kind of harmonious equilibrium may become more intense. Whether hope and despair reside in us side by side, evenly balanced at a particular time, or one dominates, or they alternate over time, they are emotions that require our attention if we are to come to terms with aging.

It can be helpful to see these feelings as on a continuum, with abject despair on one end and unbridled hope on the other. A person's place on the continuum may be constant or may fluctuate greatly. The proportions of hope and hopefulness may vary from moment to moment. You can have a go at taking your own "temperature" and see where you come out. The midpoint might represent a standoff between the two. Or hope and hopelessness may not be things that you feel at a particular time or in a particular situation. But one could argue that some modicum of hope must exist for us to soldier on even when that hope is laced with degrees of despair. Also, hopefulness or hopelessness may be a generalized mood, pervading our entire orientation toward life, or it may be a particular affect directed toward a specific person, event, or condition at a given time.

What is the experience of despair, of hopelessness? It's a sense that the present is bleak and that not much good will happen now or in the future. It is a feeling of gloom pervading the universe. It is a surrender to inner darkness and a sad, depressed feeling. You believe that fate is against you and that you can't do much to change the consequences of misfortunes that have already descended on you and that you expect to continue and worsen in the future.

On the other hand, hope is the faith and expectation that something desirable will happen to you—that something you wish for will come to you. It may come purely by chance, or you may bring it about by your own efforts. Hope is the belief that certain wishes are attainable. Hope fills your life with brightness, zest, eagerness, and a forward-looking attitude. Hope enables you to keep on—to continue fighting, resisting, and working against the stacked odds. It enables you to not accept defeat in difficult situations. It motivates you to try to prevail by inspiring confidence in a beneficent future. Where the despairing side says, "Why bother? It isn't worth it" and is ready to give up, the hopeful side believes that things will change, that positive possibilities will blossom into actualities. Hope is associated with the life force and produces the exertion of will and determination not to give in to adversity. Whereas despair says, "Give up," hope says, "Hold on." With despair, everything is too hard. With hope, you feel that you can and will endure. In despair, you might surrender to a passive life that is a form of death. With hope, life pulsates in an uninterrupted stream of ongoing actions.

These comparative charts contrast the differences between hope and despair. If the hopeful side and the despairing side were to carry on a dialogue, here's what they might say:

HOPE	DESPAIR
I haven't had enough of life. I want more. My life is not over.	*I've had enough and I'm ready to give up. I feel my life is over.*
I can manage and stay in control.	*I feel overwhelmed.*
I want to stay related to people.	*I have no desire to see others.*

It's never too late to start something new. I try to expand my interests and pursuits.

It's too late for anything and everything. I live day-to-day with no direction and nothing to do.

I feel vital, energetic, and enthusiastic.

I feel old, tired, spent, and depressed.

Life is different from what it was, but it is still good and continues to be worth living.

Anything good that ever happened to me is in the past. The future will be that way too: bleak and unappetizing.

I will try to keep on making this a good life, and make my life meaningful.

There is nothing in it for me.

I can't wait to get up in the morning and get involved in a project I've been working on.

Oh God, how I hate to get up and face the day. Let me sleep a little longer.

I don't have enough time to do everything I want to do.	*I have no wish or desire to do anything. Life is dull and tasteless.*
I'm intensely interested and involved in life, with opportunities to explore all kinds of things.	*This is the worst time of life, and I can't do anything about it. Nothing can or will help me, and I can't do anything to make my life worthwhile, meaningful, or useful.*
I'm never bored	*I've lost all appetite for life. It's not worth doing anything. I'm always bored. I can't arouse an interest in anything.*
I want to continue to change and grow.	*I've gone as far as I can, and I don't want to put any more effort into changing my ways.*

I feel that I matter to someone and am contributing in
some way to others.

*I don't matter to anyone,
and no one and nothing
matters to me.*

The future holds little fear
for me, and I am secure
about it.

*I am frightened and
helpless and fear the
future. I feel completely at
its mercy.*

I take care of myself and
take care not to hurt
myself. I keep in shape,
physically and mentally.

*I carelessly get hurt,
physically or emotionally.
I let myself deteriorate
without trying to stop it.*

Older age is a time of
transition to the new and
unexpected. Each day
brings new possibilities
and opportunities for
relationships, thoughts,
feelings, experiences,
understandings, and
discoveries.

*Old age is a time
of stagnation and
deterioration. Old age
is the end. It holds no
promises, no attractions,
just inevitable dreariness,
emptiness, and
bleakness.*

My energy flows easily and readily. I try to maintain a positive attitude despite illness and adversity	*I am tired and sad. I feel too heavy and too disgusted with life. Illness and adversity determine my mood. They are usually dark and overwhelm me.*
I try to expand my interests and pursuits. I have purposes, causes, projects to work on and to work for.	*I constrict and limit my interests and pursuits. I live day to day with no direction and little or nothing to do.*
I am usually optimistic and enthusiastic.	*I am usually pessimistic and depressed.*

DESPAIR: WHERE WE GET IT

The sources of despair are easier to identify than those of hope. It's a long list. Despair can begin with a difficult, painful, and disturbing upbringing; illness or other misfortunes and adversities; a biological predisposition; a depressed emotional state; fear of death; disillusionment about a person, situation, or relationship because of betrayal or abandonment by an intimate; or the death of a parent, spouse, or child.

Psychological or physical decline or dysfunction can bring us to the depths of despair, as can loneliness, fatigue, inaction, or action that we find purposeless and useless.

Of course, the above are not all the possible sources of hopelessness, nor does any one of them necessarily bring us to despair.

I recall, at the height of my struggle with asthma, trying to fight off despair about ever getting back to a place where I was content with my functioning and my feelings. I remember the pull just to "give up"—surrender to the illness and sink into inactivity, depression, and minimal existence. I also remember the small voice in me saying, *No, I will not quit. I'm going to fight to regain my foothold on life. If I can't control the illness, I'm not going to let it control my moods, attitudes, and emotional states.* As it became more difficult for me, I became more determined to learn something, to derive some benefit from this misery. As my despondency alternated with hopefulness, it became clear to me that a fierce struggle was going on within me over the question *Do I want to live, or die?* Although one part of me was ready to accept death rather than continue with the suffering, another part, just a bit stronger, wasn't ready to go and was opting for life. This larger

struggle—whether my dominant emotional orientation to life and living would be hopefulness, or despair,
fighting for life or giving up on it—also involved an
associated contest between hope and despair, which
went on from one moment to the next. As I watched
the variations and alterations in my breathing, the
lightness or heaviness of the inhalations and exhala-
tions, the tightness or looseness of my chest, the energy
losses and the energy increases; as I was overcome by
the fear of an asthmatic attack that would immobilize
me at any moment, and when that passed, feeling at
the next moment confident that nothing serious would
happen, each of these signs of greater or lesser stress
was accompanied by leaping hope or desolation and
despondency. If the sign was negative (i.e., my chest
was tight and the phlegm was stuck and I couldn't
clear it out and I was wheezing noticeably), I would
plummet into despair. In the next moment or hour,
when my chest was loose and the wheeze was gone, I
would become hopeful again, confident that I would
lick the illness. As multiple symptoms accumulated at
a particular time, I anticipated continuing deterioration until eventually I would become a "basket case."
As these symptoms receded and I had an hour a day
of relief (or at least less distress), I experienced an in-
jection of hope. I observed the waxing and waning
of hope and despair, this oscillation between fearing

the worst and expecting something good. I began to develop a bit of distance and detachment from the affects and processes that brought them about. I began to observe the patterns and variations and to derive some satisfaction in becoming more aware of how and when my reactions of hope and hopelessness occurred. By becoming an observer, I slowly began to feel I was gaining some control over my despair regardless of my physical condition.

HOPEFULNESS AND WHERE TO FIND IT

We need to recognize the sources of hopefulness and seek them out.

Here are just a few:

- good fortune of various kinds

- a genetic predisposition toward happiness

- the arrival of grandchildren

- associates who are full of hope, who can serve as models to emulate

- spiritual faith

- learning about contexts and circumstances that are hope-inducing, such as brave and noble deeds (for example, a community working together to hide Jews from the Nazis, or an organization dedicated to stop the poaching of endangered species)

- being inspired by constructive and creative actions on the part of others, or by a struggle that succeeds against daunting odds

- keeping an attachment to someone younger than yourself whose growth and development you have a passionate interest and investment in

- a fulfilling and satisfying personal and social environment

- a loving upbringing

- previous success in any arena

- continued involvement in activities that are meaningful to you

- continued loving relations with one or more people

How do we evoke hopefulness where it isn't? How do we get it to predominate over despair when both are present? And how do we reinforce hope so it continues to play a more central role than hopelessness in our lives? When despair is present in a powerful way, how can we learn to use it to strengthen ourselves while at the same time embracing or resisting it? How can we learn how to abandon or transform it? Finally, how can we best combine and balance these two sides? The beauty of keeping up hope as a continuing orientation lies in the fact that it is a manifestation of faith in life, in ourselves, and in other people. In the broadest sense, this implies a belief that our hope, as manifested in our persistent efforts, can move us toward self-healing, a more caring community, and a better world.

Whether you can pursue the three goals I have suggested—coming to terms with your issues, aging well, and becoming the best person you can be—will depend greatly on the balance between your energetic, hopeful life force and your enervating despair force. Which one is predominating in your battle to lead a good and rewarding later life? This basic tension underlies and influences all the other dilemmas we've discussed above. The way you resolve it will have a continuing effect on your life.

If the tensions, conflicts, and tug-of-war between your opposite orientations are prolonged, intense, and unresolved, they may dominate your mood and drain your energy. This would prevent you from pursuing an improved quality of life as vigorously and as fully as you can. Thus, it is crucial to find equilibrium and come to terms with these dilemmas as well and as quickly as you can. Here's how I suggest going about it:

Engage life actively and fully; face reality (as much as you can); be as self-reliant as you can; be hopeful and optimistic about the future; maintain intimate relations, yet seek solitude when you need it; use your energy for a project that keeps you involved in the world. Resist the pull toward passivity, isolation, and withdrawal from your community. Avoid dependency as much as you can, but let yourself be dependent when you need to be. Overcome despair, and find hopefulness in every way that you can.

FOUR

Expanding Our Awareness

Our freedom extends only as far
as our consciousness reaches.
—Carl Jung in *Alchemical Studies*

Many of the tools that we need in order to age well and become the best people we can be may be summed up in one word: awareness. When we expand our awareness, we can identify our problem areas, think about solutions, and go for our objectives. In this chapter, we'll discuss some of the ways that we can expand our consciousness and apply that greater awareness to making our later years the best they can be.

One of the most significant ways that we are different from all other animals is our capacity to think about ourselves, about others, and about what we've seen. That is, we can be both *self*-reflective and reflective about the world outside ourselves. We have the capacity to think in ever more complex ways about our lives, extending our comprehension into many realms. We can take into account the past and the future, means and ends, as well as the connections between them.

Because we all have this uniquely human capacity, we can learn to develop our awareness and become more conscious of the impact that events have on us. We can become more careful and acute observers of outside events. We can also learn to perceive our own thoughts, feelings, behaviors, and interactions more clearly.

We sleepwalk through too much of life, half-aware, on autopilot! Yet we can be so much more conscious of what is happening to us.

Huston Smith, in his book *The World's Religions: Our Great Wisdom Traditions*, tells us that the Buddha believed "that freedom—liberation from unconscious, robot-like existence—is achieved by self-awareness. To this end, he insisted that we seek to understand ourselves in depth, seeing everything minutely, 'as it really is.'"[6]

Awareness is a unique life-preserving activity without which we would live a poorer life, or no life at all. All of us are aware to some degree, yet we all have the potential to grow in awareness. Of course, there are also things that interfere with our becoming more aware. Distractions, absentmindedness, and preoccupation can all hinder our

6 Huston Smith, *The World's Religions* (New York: HarperCollins, 1991), 110

efforts to expand our awareness. Such expansion might also go against the grain of long-standing habits. But by continuing to work at it, we can reap many benefits.

Expanded awareness can help us to . . .

> . . . grow in wisdom and positive humanity;

> . . . increase our curiosity, excitement, and involvement in life;

> . . . sharpen our observations and deepen our understanding of our mental states, our bodies, our functioning, our relationships, and our experiences;

> . . . see more clearly the connections between our inner and outer realities;

> . . . recognize more readily the ageism and age-casting we encounter;

> . . . empower ourselves to create the identities we want;

. . . gain more control over what
happens to us;

. . . resist some of the negative
tendencies of aging, such as passivity,
mindlessness, and boredom;

. . . cope with difficulties by gaining
insight into the nature of our aging selves;

. . . become more empathic;

. . . improve our self-esteem through
greater clarity and comprehension
about ourselves;

. . . reestablish our equilibrium when
we are off balance;

. . . see who we are now, and
compare that person with who we
want to become.

So how do we get this expanded awareness? Perhaps a
good place to begin is with the timeworn instruction
to "Stop, look, and listen." "Stop" means prepare to pay
attention. "Look" and "listen" mean try various ways to

observe mindfully and penetrate the realities confronting us. Thus, expanding our awareness is a process that moves us from an unfocused, preoccupied, or careless consciousness to one that is directed, thoughtful, and focused. Such consciousness nurtures sensitivity to what is happening in us and around us, as well as to what we ourselves are doing. Of course, we usually undertake this process unconsciously, giving it little or no thought. But we can make this process more conscious, fuller, and take it beyond the merely habitual.

What follows are methods of expanding awareness that have helped me personally and that anyone can benefit from. Try the ones that appeal to you, in any order that feels right. After a bit of practice, you just might become enthusiastic about working at it.

LOOKING ON

We can *gaze* at a scene in a relaxed, leisurely fashion, just enjoying it. We can pay attention to color and movement in our peripheral vision as well as to the image that is in sharper focus. We can *scan* a social scene to select from it what is interesting, threatening, or important to us. Here the idea is to intuitively absorb the totality of what we are confronting—try to grasp the whole. The context and details will subsequently come into focus. Looking on involves following the continuous flow of events as much as we can, and appreciating their full sweep.

Japan

I am in a garden in Japan. I am awestruck with the beauty and am breathless trying to absorb it. There is so much to take in: an unusual pond, flowers in great profusion, bushes of unusual shapes and design, an atmosphere that is hard to define, arrangements of owers and bushes, delicately placed. After the scene stabilizes in my mind, I watch myself trying to come to terms with this magical scene. I wonder why this is so rare an experience. I would like to stay longer in Kyoto but can't. What a pity!

LOOKING OUT

Looking on prepared us for looking outward. Looking out, we watch what is out there in all its detail, bringing it into focus and seeing it as clearly and accurately as we can. The more we see, the more we may want to see, and the more adept we get at observing.

We can carefully notice what others are doing in relation to us, and vice versa, paying attention to the objects and people in the situation (including ourselves). We can also pay attention to the interaction between us and them. If too much is going on, we can focus on what appears to us to be important.

We can attend intuitively to what we've noticed, and consciously take it in as much as possible. Looking out also means seeing how, when, and where it affects us.

THE NEW YORK SUBWAY
Every time I come to New York, my fear rises. So much violence! So many stories about violence. When I enter the subway and stand on a platform waiting for a train, I scan the scene. (How many people are here? Who are they? What do they look like? What are they carrying? Where are they located with reference to me?

Close or far away? Do any of them look dangerous?) Then I focus on one person or a group who might be . . . what? Aggressors? Attackers? Thieves? I keep my eye on them. What are they doing? In what direction are they moving? Do they give any signs of being ready to act in other ways than the conventional ways that subway patrons behave? I try to notice the slightest hints or subtle cues of readiness to act aggressively. I also pay attention to my own inner states. How alert am I? Has my fear grown so big that it is beginning to immobilize me? Does this make it harder to observe? I try to listen to the voices and faces of the persons I've focused on. Are they engaged in false, that is, deceptive jocularity? Can I detect a threatening note in what they say and how they say it? How are they dressed? Can I detect

CONCEALED WEAPONS? HOW ARE THE OTHERS ON THE PLATFORM REACTING TO THEM? HOW ARE THE "IDENTIFIED ONES" MOVING ABOUT? WHERE TO? THEN I BEGIN TO ASK QUESTIONS OF MYSELF: AM I BEING OVERLY CAUTIOUS OR NOT CAUTIOUS ENOUGH? DO I EXAGGERATE WHAT I SEE, OR UNDERVALUE MY OBSERVATIONS? I MOVE BACK AND FORTH BETWEEN WHAT I PERCEIVE IN THE MOVEMENTS OF THE OTHER PEOPLE, AND HOW I RESPOND INWARDLY. THIS ALL HAPPENS VERY QUICKLY. WHEN THE TRAIN ARRIVES, AND "THEY" DO NOT ENTER THE TRAIN WITH ME, MY TENSION BREAKS AND I RELAX, DROPPING MY ACUTE VIGILANCE.

ON THE TRAIN, I CARRY ON A CONVERSATION WITH MYSELF. WAS I BEING FOOLISH, OR REALISTIC? WAS IT REASONABLE TO BE SO CAUTIOUS AND FEARFUL, OR WAS IT JUST A FALSE READING OF THE NEW YORK SUBWAYS, AT LEAST IN THIS SITUATION AND AT THIS TIME? WAS I TENSE BECAUSE I AM COWARDLY,

OR DID I HAVE GOOD REASON TO WATCH
CAREFULLY FOR POSSIBLE TROUBLE? WILL
ALL THIS AWARENESS REALLY BE OF HELP
IF AN ATTACK OCCURS, OR IS THIS JUST
ABOUT MY NEED TO FEEL PREPARED?
THEN I FEEL A LITTLE GUILTY, HAVING
THESE SUSPICIOUS THOUGHTS ABOUT
INNOCENT STRANGERS WHO MAY INTEND
ME NO HARM WHATEVER. WHAT HAVE I
LEARNED AS A RESULT OF THE SITUATION?
WILL I BE BETTER PREPARED NEXT
TIME? I LEAVE THE SCENE FEELING THAT
I'D RATHER LOOK TO MY OWN SAFETY
THAN BE SORRY LATER.

LOOKING IN

This is where we see into a situation, concentrating intently to get to the core of what we are beholding. Here, we try to open ourselves up, use all our five senses, our kinesthetic sense, and our *intuitive* sense of our experience. This means being fully present and listening carefully and intently to the words, voice, and nuances of what we hear, as well as what the speaker might mean or intend. It also means that we feel the affective tone—the emotional intensity or flatness—of what is being communicated. Initially, what we are observing may appear vague or confusing or leave us with unclear impressions. But with more experience breaking situations down into their constituent parts, our impressions may become clearer and their outlines sharper. Eventually, we begin to see the movements, interactions, and coherence or incoherence while they are occurring.

Besides penetrating an outward situation, looking in also involves observing our own reactions to the situation, and our own inner state. In this way, we perceive what we've observed and we filter our observations through our heart and mind, seeing and registering their significance for us. Then we keep looking inside to observe our thoughts, feelings, bodily sensations, attitudes, perceptions, and vague understandings that have occurred as we observed the scene. These flash in and out of our awareness, then become fixed and, finally, assimilated and converted into our experience.

My Body

As a consequence of dealing with my asthma, I often focus on my body. I need to be aware of my body, given my

NEED TO INHALE FROM A BRONCHODILATOR EVERY SIX HOURS, TAKE ANOTHER SPRAY TWICE A DAY, AND SWALLOW A DAILY STEROID PILL. DESPITE THE NECESSARY PREOCCUPATION WITH THESE TREATMENTS, I OFTEN TAKE A DETACHED, CURIOUS, AND INVESTIGATORY LOOK AT WHAT IS HAPPENING TO ME. I NOTICE THAT THE STEROIDS HAVE CAUSED MANY CONSPICUOUS BRUISES TO APPEAR EASILY FROM CONTACT BETWEEN MY ARM AND A HARD OBJECT. I HAVE THESE VERY BRIGHT SPOTS ON THE BACK OF MY HAND AND ARMS AS A CONSEQUENCE OF THESE CONTACTS.

AND THESE UGLY BRUISES ON MY SKIN, PEPPER RED AND ROSE, BIG AND SMALL—I LOVE THEM ALL IN SOME WAY, STANDING OUT AGAINST THE REST OF MY ARM. WHAT TELLTALE SIGNS OF TOO MANY STEROIDS IN THE SYSTEM! YET THERE IS SOMETHING APPEALING ABOUT THEM. THE BRUISES ARE DIFFERENT FROM THE REST OF MY SKIN, AND IN ISOLATION THEY REPRESENT THE OUTSIDER, THAT SIDE OF ME THAT I also cherish. So I don't object too much. Besides, I know they will go away in good time. While they're here, they make for some interesting decorations on what is otherwise a dull-looking arm.

Also, ashes momentarily appear before my eyes, and I hear myself wheezing, whistling, and breathing heavily. It is both strange and familiar to me. I experience a tension between being fearful of what I see, hear, feel, and intuit and being curious about what it is all about. It is fascinating to watch my body as it undergoes small changes. As much as I can, I try to work out satisfactory solutions to these changes. Puffing and panting on exertion, shortness of breath, exhaustion after a slight effort— all are signs that danger is approaching. Even though the time consumed taking medications is not

GREAT, HAVING TO BE CONCERNED AND
PREOCCUPIED WITH IT ANNOYS ME.

Every COLD BRINGS AN INFECTION,
FOLLOWED BY DIFFICULTY IN COUGHING UP
PHLEGM, SINCE IT IS DEEP WITHIN THE
LUNGS. The STRUGGLE TO COUGH IT UP
MAY GO ON FOR A FEW MINUTES OR FOR
HALF AN HOUR. There IS A CURIOUS POINT
AND COUNTERPOINT TO THE COUGH, THE
RELEASE OF PHLEGM, ANOTHER COUGH,
ANOTHER RELEASE OF MORE PHLEGM,
UNTIL MY LUNGS FINALLY FEEL CLEAR. It
IS A SLOW PROCESS, AND I AM EXHAUSTED
BY THE END OF IT. The MORE I COUGH
WITH JUST A SMALL RESULT, THE MORE
TIRED I GET AND THE LESS EFFECTIVE
I GET AT BRINGING IT UP, AND THE
MORE WORRIED I GET. The MORE TIRED
I GET, THE LESS ENERGY I HAVE FOR
COUGHING. Every LITTLE BIT THAT COMES
UP HELPS THE   OW OF AIR INTO MY
LUNGS, BUT I KNOW I'VE GOTTEN IT ALL
WHEN I NO LONGER RASP AND COUGH
AND WHEN I FEEL THE CLEAN, CLEAR
AIR GOING THROUGH MY LUNGS WITHOUT

INTERRUPTION. THEN I EXPERIENCE RELIEF AND RECOGNIZE HOW HELPFUL AND FASCINATING IT IS TO NOTE THIS PROCESS AND WRITE IT DOWN. IT MITIGATES SOME OF THE DISCOMFORT BY OBJECTIFYING IT ON PAPER. WRITING, I SEE MYSELF AND THE ENTIRE EXPERIENCE RETROSPECTIVELY, AND THAT IS A DIFFERENT EXPERIENCE FROM THE ACTUAL ONE THAT I'VE GONE THROUGH. OBSERVING AND WRITING IT DOWN HELPS ME KEEP MY EQUILIBRIUM.

OBSERVING MYSELF AND MAKING NOTES BETWEEN COUGHS HELPS. IN THIS WAY, I GIVE EQUAL TIME TO THE WRITING AND TO THE STRUGGLE. IT ISN'T EASY TO FIND TIME FOR NOTE-TAKING BETWEEN COUGHS OR RIGHT AFTERWARD. I ALSO OBSERVE THAT MUCH FATIGUE IS ASSOCIATED WITH THE STRUGGLE, WHICH LEADS ME TO THINK, THIS IS HOW IT MUST BE TO BE VERY, VERY OLD—ANCIENT. I OBSERVE, TOO, THAT I'M GETTING SOME SATISFACTION OUT OF PREVAILING IN THIS STRUGGLE. DESPITE THE SHORTNESS OF BREATH AND THE ANXIETY ABOUT MY

CONGESTED LUNGS, IT IS SATISFYING TO FEEL THAT I STILL HAVE THE STRENGTH, THE WILL, AND THE POWER TO CONTINUE THE FIGHT AND THAT I WON'T LIE DOWN AND SURRENDER. THE STRUGGLE IS AS IMPORTANT AS THE VICTORY, FOR IN THAT STRUGGLE I EXPERIENCE MY OWN LIFE ENERGY ALSO STRUGGLING TO EMERGE MORE STRONGLY AND MAINTAIN ITSELF. IF I CAN STAY INVOLVED AND COMMITTED TO THE PROCESS AS IT ARISES AND RECEDES, THE RESULTS THAT I WANT MAY TAKE CARE OF THEMSELVES.

AND I KNOW THAT ANY VICTORY IS ONLY A TEMPORARY ONE. ANOTHER STRUGGLE WILL COME, AND ANOTHER, INDEFINITELY UNTIL THERE ARE NO MORE, AND IN BETWEEN STRUGGLES I WILL CONTINUE TO LIVE AS ENTHUSIASTICALLY AS I CAN.

REFLECTION

Reflexive attention can follow our observations. At the time an event occurs, it can be difficult for us to sort it

out, absorb it fully, fathom its deeper meaning, or identify its connections with other events and experiences. It
is only after the fact that we can really begin to extract
its full significance. We might try to bring to the surface
the ideas and thoughts that are present at the outer edges
of our memory, to see what new information comes in
from the periphery of our awareness. After observing
an event, situation, or relationship, it's good to reflect
on the nature and processes of our awareness. At this
point, we can become invested in those processes. We
also might begin to recognize that we filter our insights
and feelings through interpretive lenses that both enable
and restrict our vision and awareness. If we are to develop our awareness more clearly, accurately, and fully,
we must try to recognize and transcend the limitations
that we all are subject to. It is no easy task.

REFLECTION OCCURS WHEN WE:

Observe our observations. We can look at ourselves and visualize in our imagination what we
previously observed, and try to remember and
reconstitute the scene. We should try to identify
what we might have distorted or misrepresented.
We need to ask ourselves: How accurate are my
observations, and in what areas are the inaccura-
cies apt to occur? What did I miss, and how can

I tell what I missed? When reviewing my observations, do things come flooding in from my peripheral vision that I hadn't really noticed before?

Look at our looking. How did we experience our looking? Did anything interrupt, divert, or curtail it? Is what we saw enough of a representation of what happened? Can we see ourselves looking at the scene? What do we look like in our mind's eye?

Notice ourselves noticing. Imagine or capture the image of ourselves as we notice what is happening outside us. Is our mode of noticing sufficient for the occasion? What are we taking in as we notice, and how do we feel about our noticing?

Sense our sensing. Could our sense impressions, body signals, and intuitions flower under the circumstances? If not, can we now fill them out after the fact?

Listen to our listening. Were the sounds clear and distinguishable? Did we get the communication right? How might we have distorted the words and communication? Can we see alternative interpretations from the ones that we made? Can we fill in the blank spaces if any exist?

Concentrate on our concentration. Can we closely examine and evaluate how firm and focused our concentration was? Did it wander? If there were interferences, were we able to do anything about them? Can we improve our concentration by exercise and practice?

React to our reactions. How do we feel now about our reactions? Were they appropriate and consonant with the scene and what happened? Or did they interfere with the full flow of our awareness?

Perceive our perceptions. Do we now believe that the transformation from outside event to inner experience, the way we filtered and absorbed these outside events, is valid? Do we have any doubts about our representation of them in our inner understanding?

Experience our experiences. Looking at ourselves now as the person who had those experiences then, do they seem "right"? Was it us who had the experiences, and are those experiences actually the ones we had? What is the nature of our feelings, thoughts, and insights as we review our experiences?

Feel our feelings. Are the feelings we had then the ones we would now identify as having had at that time? Would we add anything to our feelings? Would we describe them in the same way? Or would we change our description?

Be aware of our awareness. What do we now know about the awareness we have developed of any particular event or scene we observed? Does it stay with us now as *the awareness* we will take away with us? Do we see room for expansion, and can we think of ways to expand our awareness?

An Accident

I see an accident on the street. Someone is hurt. I don't look carefully, because it is too painful. I force myself to look. It seems that a young man has flipped over the front of his motorcycle and broken his knee. People around him try to help. I'm in my car in traffic and wait to see what happens. An ambulance comes soon to take him off. I recognize the apprehension and the sickly feeling

THAT IS BEGINNING TO ARISE IN ME. I BEGIN TO WORRY ABOUT MY SON, WHO IS TRAVELING IN TIBET, AND SUDDENLY GET THE FEELING THAT HE IS UNSAFE AND MIGHT BE HURT. I FANTASIZE ABOUT ALL THE THINGS THAT CAN HAPPEN TO HIM. HE'S IN A TRUCK ON A NARROW MOUNTAIN ROAD AND IT GOES OVER THE SIDE. HE'S IN A REMOTE AREA AND ATTACKED BY THIEVES. HE'S ALONE IN AN ISOLATED AREA AND FALLS AND BREAKS HIS ANKLE, AND THERE'S NO ONE AROUND TO HELP HIM. I SUDDENLY STOP MY FANTASIES AND LOOK BACK AT ALL THE HORRIBLE THINGS I'VE IMAGINED, SAYING TO MYSELF, "LOOK AT YOU, CREATING THESE DISTURBING FANTASIES! WHY HAVE YOU DONE THIS? STOP IT." I DO, AND I WONDER WHY I HAVE GOTTEN MYSELF IN THIS MOOD OF DREAD AND APPREHENSION.

The challenge of expanding our awareness is to push ourselves to the outer edge of our awareness so that we might move beyond it. Further, the challenge is to note to ourselves more acutely and with greater depth what we are doing, thinking, and feeling as we move along in our daily activities.

REMEMBERING

The threat of forgetting is always present especially when we are trying hard to remember something. Here are some techniques for remembering that I have found useful.

Complete tasks immediately—as soon as you think about it, if you can. Closing the gap between thinking and doing reduces the chances of forgetting.

Try to concern yourself with only one thing at a time, and keep focused on that one thing. Concentrate! And do not let extraneous thoughts, feelings, and fantasies intrude. Learn how to suspend, and practice putting aside, whatever intrudes on your current attempt to remember. You can let the intruder in after you feel secure that you will not forget, when you have written it down, or when you have finished the task at hand.

Repeat in your mind, over and over, what you wish to remember. Make a conscious note of it as you repeat it, until you can record it somewhere or you feel secure that you will not forget it, because it is so strongly emblazoned in your memory.

Double-check to make sure you've done what you think you have. Have you ever thought about doing something (for example, closing the drapes) but didn't do it, and then thought you did? Did you then later discover, much to your chagrin, that the drapes were still open? Double-checking definitely helps.

Develop techniques that help you retain what you wish to remember. For example, make notes to yourself and keep them where you are apt to be or where you can't overlook them. For another example, I know I have to take my medication at two p.m. If I remember this at one p.m., I put the medication in front of me so that it is staring me in the face.

And finally, a word on patience. When you forget something you want to remember, wait. It usually doesn't come back if you try to force yourself to remember. When I wait with relaxed anticipation, or surrender to the idea that "it will come later," the forgotten thought usually springs forth spontaneously at a later time.

OBJECTIVITY AND DETACHMENT

Although we say we would like to be completely objective, excluding all biases from our perceptions, it is impossible to do so. We cannot be fully objective about ourselves. Nor can we eliminate bias from our perceptions of our intimates, our relationships, the events we observe, and our social world. But that's no reason to despair of ever becoming more objective than we already are. We can try to discover and reduce our preconceptions and predisposition to see things in a certain way. We can try to make our observations and interpretations less influenced by self-interest and freer of our tendencies to react cognitively in a habitual way.

Thus, to make our awareness correspond more to reality as it is, we must try to free ourselves as much as we can from our biases, stereotypes, and habitual distortions. We especially need to become more aware of the ways that our culture predisposes us to particular interpretations and understandings.

Our culture provides us with lenses that we see the world through. These lenses can be wide-angle or narrow, sharply focused or hazy, microscopic or telescopic, thus reducing, enlarging, obscuring, or clarifying our perceptions. Although we cannot function without these lenses, they are unavoidably clouded by preconceptions and prejudices, inhibitions, and the many limitations imposed on us by our cultural conditioning. If we are to develop our awareness more clearly, accurately, and fully, we must try to recognize and transcend these screens to our awareness.

It is worth struggling to attain more objectivity and detachment than we ordinarily have, in order to experience the satisfaction and power of being in closer touch with the truth.

The validity or truthfulness of what we observe, are aware of, and experience is in part dependent on the degree of detachment and objectivity we can bring to a situation. This is especially true if our values, feelings, or desires are involved. Most of us tend to see what we want to see, hear what we want to hear, find evidence for what we want to believe, react negatively to those who pose a challenge to what we believe in, and thus dismiss contrary ideas. We ordinarily take for granted that most of what is should be, and we believe that we are being objective when we see phenomena from the perspective of conventional, accepted knowledge.

Don't be afraid to entertain a perspective that is very different from our own, strange and daring though it may seem. Even if nothing comes of it, after consideration and examination we might be able to stretch our mind, enlarge our vision, entertain possibilities previously unknown, and stimulate our imagination to see "another side."

Clark Clifford, in his *New Yorker* article of April 1, 1991, indicates one way of trying to be more objective:

> *Kennedy was unusually successful in maintaining objectivity under pressure. I felt on occasion that as he dealt with personal and professional crises he was able to step away from himself and look at a problem as though it involved someone else.*

Sometimes watching him during a discussion of some contentious issue, I felt as if Kennedy's mind had left his body to observe the proceedings with a detached, almost amused air. Something within him seemed to be saying, "This may seem supremely—even transcendently—important right now, but will it matter in fifty years? In one year? I must not permit myself to become involved to the point where my judgment is suspect."[7]

We become more objective and reduce our biases when we make the effort to . . .

> . . . be less judgmental and evaluative of other people's behavior. Then we can see it more clearly for what it is.

> . . . commit ourselves to search out the truth in a situation, even if it is not in our self-interest.

> . . . discover our biases and push them back, or take them into

7 Clark Clifford and Richard Holbrooke, "Serving the President: The Truman Years—II," *New Yorker*, April 1, 1991, 67.

account, when becoming aware of a situation, interaction, or relationship.

. . . suspend and question, if only temporarily, the beliefs that we feel dogmatically certain about. See how it would feel to believe otherwise, and what consequences might emerge.

. . . detach ourselves from our own convictions when another has a set of completely opposite beliefs. Acknowledge and accept these opposing values as being potentially just as legitimate as our own, even though they differ so radically. Listen intently and carefully to this opposing view to absorb its meaning and intention. Even if our minds aren't changed, we may appreciate or respect the other person's position more than before.

. . . systematically recount to ourselves the ways that our culture has conditioned us: our taken-for-granted ways of thinking and feeling; what we think is valuable;

our assumptions about human nature and the human condition, how we should live our lives, and the constraints we need to exercise. Identify this cultural conditioning and become as fully aware of it as you can. Articulate it to yourself and ask if you really accept all of it, and why. Then try to transcend whatever is unacceptable or questionable.

. . . where there are a number of different viewpoints in a many-sided discussion or debate, to "try on" each point of view by comparing it with our own as dispassionately as possible. Then try to argue from each of these perspectives to discover how it affects your own thinking and feeling.

. . . sympathetically compare the values and ideology of another culture that is quite different from our own. Then try to reconcile the differences or justify maintaining our cultural values.

. . . imagine alternatives to the usual way we view a situation, and to the worldview that we bring to it.

. . . detach from ourselves and the situations we are in. We must stand outside ourselves and look at ourselves and our beliefs as if we were someone else.

My Class

I TEACH A CLASS IN WHICH ALL THE STUDENTS HAVE COMMITTED THEMSELVES TO ATTEND EVERY SESSION AND TO LET ME KNOW BEFORE THE CLASS STARTS IF IT IS IMPOSSIBLE TO DO SO. A STUDENT IS ABSENT AND DOESN'T CALL ME. I'M QUITE ANNOYED WITH HER, AND WHEN SHE ARRIVES FOR THE NEXT SESSION, I AM FOCUSED ON WHY SHE MISSED THE CLASS, AND ASK HER ABOUT IT. SHE TELLS ME THAT HER MOTHER HAD DIED. I REPLY, "THAT'S OKAY, THEN." (MEANING THAT HER REASONS FOR MISSING THE CLASS WERE ACCEPTABLE.)

No sooner were the words out of my mouth than I recognized how unfeeling, cold, and dehumanizing my remark was. I quickly apologized and offered my condolences. I then reflected on how narrow and restricted my attitude and response were, and wondered what led me to put the teacher response before the human response. I concluded that I had been too concerned about maintaining the rules and being the authority who enforces them, rather than responding on a human level. I didn't like myself for the response and vowed never to let it happen again.

PERSPECTIVE

Because we have lived a long time, years of experience inform our awareness, thought, and understanding. We have been wizened and toughened by crises confronted and resolved, by a sense of how things work out over time, by the difficulties and surprises that unpredictably occur, and by our understanding of the fragility and uncertainty of life. In our most serious and contemplative moments, we can crystallize a philosophical perspective that informs our lives. It can penetrate our immediate life situation and the context it occurs in; influence the way we look at ourselves, others, and the universe; and help us interpret all these things. This perspective can help us see beyond and beneath things that happen. It provides a vantage point, a frame of reference, to view our life and our world. Thus, a broad and deep perspective might help us . . .

> . . . distinguish the ephemeral, temporary, and superficial from profound, more permanent values, beliefs, and modes of behavior.

> . . . become more fully aware of the chain of generational continuity and see ourselves as vehicles and way stations in the course of human evolution.

> . . . develop insight into the connectedness and the poignancy of life and death.

. . . accept and appreciate life's intricacies and complexities, and also its simplicities.

. . . see the mixture of child and adult that exists in each of us.

. . . contemplate the role of chance and accident in determining our fate.

. . . appreciate the continuity of the human race even though no single individual lives indefinitely.

. . . understand ourselves as part of a larger whole—one humanity—and see how we contribute in a small way to that whole.

. . . ponder whether we have a destiny and, if so, what it is.

. . . look beneath the surface of a person, situation, or relationship and understand what is there and what is genuine.

. . . understand something about life's possibilities and limitations.

. . . enlarge our vision beyond our immediate range, focusing not only on our local area and concerns, but also on the world's concerns.

. . . develop a more inclusive and encompassing view of the interdependence of life on this planet, especially between ourselves and nature.

. . . stretch our imagination to think of original and creative ideas on matters that interest us.

. . . take a historical as well as a cross-cultural point of view, seeing the present as it relates to the past, and seeing our own culture in relation to other cultures.

. . . take a cosmic view, seeing ourselves not only in human history, but also in the history of the planets and the universe.

> . . . identify fundamental principles
> and universal truths about human
> behavior, and develop a morality that
> we can respect and embody.

A deep and long-range perspective may stretch the boundaries of our personhood and make an important contribution to our evolving character.

Maryann, 79, sees life as a series of accidental, informal events, which were precipitated by small happenings that snowballed into something significant, enlarging her humanity and wisdom. Thus, from her perspective, chance, small things, and unexpected happenings are the most significant things in shaping a life and determining its direction.

MEDITATION AND PRAYER

Spending a little time each day in meditation or prayer can expand our awareness greatly. There are many types of meditation that can help us calm the mind and enhance our concentration. What most of them have in common is a period of quiet sitting, when we practice stilling our minds and focusing on something constant, such as our breathing or a mantra. Such mental practice, especially if done daily, can have far-reaching benefits.

Dr. Herbert Benson, at Harvard Medical School, has done a great deal of research on the health-enhancing results of meditation. Apart from our felt experience of being calmed, refreshed, and relaxed, our brain waves actually change during meditation, helping improve a wide range of health conditions, from headaches to high blood pressure. Using a modified form of meditation, which Dr. Benson calls "the Relaxation Response," he reports, "A young man, who suffered from severe anxiety attacks, reports that he often felt fearful, nervous, and shaky, tense and worried. After practicing the Relaxation Response for two months, he rarely suffered from attacks of anxiety . . . In short, he felt that the practice of the Relaxation Response significantly improved his life."[8]

Prayer is a very personal activity between oneself and a spiritual reality of one's own understanding or belief. A brief period of prayer, whether daily or less frequently, can calm our mind and spirit and help us

8 Herbert Benson, *The Relaxation Response* (New York: William Morrow and Company, 1985), 166.

feel connected with a power greater than ourselves. By calming our minds, it can help us concentrate and be present with our lives in all their complexity. By offering us spiritual connection and solace, it can expand our consciousness. Simply taking the attitude of deep receptivity and calm observation of our thoughts and feelings surrounding an issue often yields solutions and insights that we ordinarily wouldn't have thought about.

HUMOR

To be aware of the comic, the ludicrous, the amusing, and the hilariously funny situation is to manifest a certain degree of objectivity. The cultivation and expression of humor can be an end in itself, as well as a form of objectivity. When we joke about something, especially about ourselves, we can detach from it and laugh at ourselves. Such experiences open up the possibility that we will see ourselves in a new light. Humor and laughter can be valuable emotional releases, making the moment joyous, sparkling, and fun. Humor can ease tension and discomfort, alleviate anxiety, lighten a heavy atmosphere. It also helps us deal with resistant and negative people. And humor in a group is a way of creating a comfortable sense of sharing in which each and all experience their common humanity.

Norman Cousins pioneered the use of laughter to heal physical ailments. He literally made himself laugh for hours a day, with the help of Marx Brothers movies, when he was in the hospital with a serious ailment. Since then, study after study has indicated that laughter improves immune functions and reduces the effects of stress. The psychological and physical benefits of laughter and joking simply cannot be overstated. Cousins writes, "It worked. I made the joyous discovery that ten minutes of genuine belly laughter had an anaesthetic effect and would give me at least two hours of pain-free sleep. When the pain-killing effect of the laughter wore off, we would switch on the motion-picture projector again and, not infrequently, it would lead to another pain-free interval."[9]

Any one of the processes described above can expand our awareness. It is important to make an effort, practice, and keep at it. The more modes we use, the greater our awareness becomes, and the greater the rewards we reap.

9 Norman Cousins, *Anatomy of an Illness as Perceived by the Patient: Reflections on Healing and Regeneration* (New York: W.W. Norton & Company, 1979), 39-40.

Morrie enjoying summer on Cape Cod.

Morrie and Rob clearing snow
at the house in Brookline, MA.

MORRIE IN CHINA, MID/1980s.

THE SCHWARTZ FAMILY 1990s:
JON, MORRIE, CHARLOTTE, ROB

MORRIE AND CHARLOTTE, EVER IN LOVE.

DAD AND HIS EFFERVESCENT PERSONALITY,
WITH ROB IN BACKGROUND.

MORRIE AND CHARLOTTE ENTERTAINING
GUESTS, AS THEY OFTEN DID.

MORRIE AND ROB DURING MORRIE'S ILLNESS.

FIVE

Ageism and Age-Casting

Ageism is a stigmatizing prejudice that denigrates older people, discriminates against us, denies our humanity, and reduces our opportunity to lead satisfying and worthwhile lives. It is a deeply laid attitude in most people. It is so unwitting and unconscious that we often don't recognize it when we are its victims, and we are just as clueless when we are its perpetrators.

I'd like to introduce the term "age-casting" to amplify the concept of ageism. It can be used to characterize the restrictions and exclusions foisted on us. We are typecast, as some actors are, into restricted stereotyped roles—specifically, the role of "old person" (and its many subsets). We are placed in a separate category of being. It is a role we are expected to play into the indefinite future—a role with negative expectations, a role that is circumscribed by belittling demands and limitations. When the stamp of disapproval in the form of ageism is added to that of age-casting, we are then burdened with identities that confine, demean, and diminish us as vital human beings and separate us from the rest of society. Thus, we are not seen as the real people we are, but as mere shadows cast by ageist projections.

But we don't have to be dominated by ageist or age-cast expectations. We can pursue our chosen goals even—or especially—if they run counter to these expectations. We, too, can be what is generally considered the province of the young: enthusiastic, lively, engaged, vital, burning with passion, forward-looking, and optimistic.

There are, of course, a number of cultural reasons why age-casting and ageism are so prevalent in our society and so deeply entrenched in most of our psyches as forms of prejudice. While we can't attribute it to any single cause, our disdain for older people probably reflects some of our culture's core values.

Individualism is still highly valued in American society. We value independence and individual initiative and, conversely, devalue dependence, which nevertheless is the reality of all of life on the planet. We know that complete independence can never really exist— we all need each other and the life systems of Earth to maintain our physical existence. Yet we strive for independence. Older people remind us of our need for each other, and the greater dependence we will all come to have if we live long enough. Eventually, we do become more dependent on family and caregivers. The American ethic of rugged individualism resists accepting this view of the future and thus contributes to a devaluation of the elderly, especially those who have become dependent.

Another factor that contributes to widespread ageism is the money-driven American society. We live in a society that values the almighty dollar above virtually all else. This includes a cultural imperative to work hard and bring home the bacon as a primary source of our self-esteem, our "worth"—especially for men. When we retire and are no longer making money, society devalues us, along with all the others who are considered failures—welfare recipients, poor people, the homeless. In many people's minds, we become inconsequential as human beings. Of course, this is ludicrous. Nobody's worth as a human being should be defined by what they earn or whether they are gainfully employed.

There may also be an existential reason: our fear of death. Old people are closer to death than most others. Thus, they remind others of that grim inevitability. We try to ignore or deny the reality of death, and therefore, we reject the reminder and harbinger of things to come. We hold up to those who are not yet old the image of what they will become—and they don't like what they see. Thus, they denigrate the messengers for forcing them to confront a message from the future.

In general, American society worships youth, and our TV culture promotes that worship and esteems superficial beauty over character.

But Henry Miller, in an interview quoted in *Songs of Experience*, offers a different vision:

> *The whole of society from time immemorial has always worshipped youth. Youth is the great word, isn't it? Now, we all know, who've been through youth, that it's far from being a glorious period in one's life. I don't know how they drummed up all those qualities that are attributed to youth. Youth has to do with spirit, not age. Men of seventy and eighty are often more youthful than the young. Theirs is the real youth. You see what I mean? It's the youth of the mind and spirit, which is everlasting.*[10]

10 Henry Miller, "Interview with Henry Miller," interview by Digby Diehl, quoted in *Songs of Experience*, by Margaret Fowler (New York: Ballantine Books, 1991), 51.

And our desire for speed and efficiency make old people obsolete, as old machines are expected to be.

Ageism and age-casting perpetrate many assaults on the selves of older people. Assaults on the self can come in different forms: humiliation or disrespect from others, denigration by them, and attacks on our dignity and worth. After enduring more than enough of these, we can readily anticipate such invalidations of ourselves and come to dread them.

Assaults on the self can come from many different directions, and ageism and age-casting may contribute to any of them. For example, someone treats us as if we were burdensome and boring. An organization doesn't want our services. A bureaucracy treats us like a number. An agency expects us to beg and grovel for a service it exists to provide. An employer fires us. It may be difficult to tell whether the bad treatment we receive is informed by ageism, or would have happened to us even if we were younger. Either way, these types of assaults on the self add up over time and may daunt us if we don't fight back.

An article in the *Boston Globe* (December 29, 1988) illustrates a severe form of ageist humiliation.

FIRED!

After more than a quarter-century of loyal endeavor, Iver Freeman was told by his company to resign. This is the story of how a 60-year-old man endured during a life soured by age discrimination and unemployment.

Iver Freeman, a 60-year-old employee of the Reed-Prentice Machinery Co. in East Longmeadow—a $75,000-a-year executive, married for 38 years, the father of three grown children—walked into work Monday, Oct. 27, 1980 and was dismissed from the company he worked for since the days of President Truman.

Freeman had seen no warning. On his left wrist he still wore the engraved watch that Package Machinery had given him several years earlier, after a quarter-century of faithful service.

He had assumed he would stay at Package Machinery until retirement, just five years away, when his friends might throw a goodbye banquet, with card and presents, and he would retire comfortably, with the pension he worked toward for so long.

Instead, Freeman received a memo, by inter-office mail, left in an envelope on his desk. "Documented event . . . make it mandatory . . . your resignation effective immediately . . . performance and attitude . . . if you require any assistance in removing your personal effects by noon."

Freeman tried to continue reading his office mail, but the lines blurred. He heard the muffled sound of his own voice telling the secretary, who was in tears, to cancel his appointments. Forever . . .

The firing distressed Freeman so much that he couldn't sleep, gained weight, spent many hours in front of the TV set, and experienced a precipitous rise in his blood pressure.

After six months his severance pay ran out. Freeman had no remaining benefits, or pension or bonuses coming to him. The unemployment people kept telling him he was over-age and over-qualified.

The Freemans had to put their condominium on the market and move to the family's small summer cottage in Harwich, on Cape Cod . . .

Iver Freeman filed a complaint with the Massachusetts Commission Against Discrimination.

People told him not to bother. The Putnam family [the owners] were well-known, they said—Roger Putnam's father had even been a mayor of Springfield and had a vocational high school named after him.

But when the commission didn't resolve the issue, Freeman filed a federal age-discrimination suit against Package Machinery in US District Court in Springfield . . .

The appellate court affirmed the judgment of $653,700 in pay and damages.

But most importantly, the court affirmed what Freeman, now 68, had come slowly, reluctantly to believe.

That the company Freeman had devoted so many years to had fired him for no other reason than that he had, in the judge's words, "seen too many summers."[11]

---

11 Barbara Carton, "Fired!" *Boston Globe*, December 20, 1988, 43.

Assaults on the self can also come from the experience of dehumanization—where others see us or treat us as if we were less than human. They act as if we were non-existent, even though we are in their company.

This type of assault has much in common with the ways that people of color and women in general are treated throughout their lives, regardless of their age, and it is equally repugnant. For older people who have been discriminated against throughout their lives for one reason or another, the dehumanizing sting of ageism has a bitterly familiar feel.

We may not always realize when ageism and age-casting are contributing to our low self-esteem, feelings of hopelessness, withdrawal, or a simple case of the "blahs." By the same token, recognizing this ageism and rejecting it in our minds and hearts can help us feel happier and stronger and renew our confidence and motivation.

If you're wondering whether you've been a victim of ageism, take a moment. Have you walked past someone who didn't respond to you, even though your presence was impossible to miss? Are there times when you are approached with indifference, "looked through," or dismissed as if you didn't matter? Are there times when you are treated as an object: something that is in the way, or something to be avoided? Have others treated you as if you were already dead, talked about you as if you were not present when you clearly were, or treated you as if you were "out of it"? Have others invalidated your experience, dismissing it as the delusion of an older person? Have you been denied access to a place or function because you are "too old"?

THE STEREOTYPES

People use a variety of terms and ideas to discriminate against older people and deny our humanity. It can be helpful to confront these stereotypes, repugnant as they are, and think about which of them are ageist and age-casting falsehoods and biases. By learning to identify ageist attitudes and language, we can more readily repudiate them in others and in ourselves.

They say we are boastful, talkative, boring, suspicious, demanding, clueless, annoying, complaining, moralizing, and a nuisance. We are rigid and set in our ways—stodgy, backward, behind the times, self-absorbed, cranky, stubborn, and inflexible. We are said to be preoccupied with ourselves, especially with our past, and to fear the future and view it as a bleak prospect. The stereotype has us as disengaged, unproductive, with nothing to do—"out of it," detached, and not oriented to modern life. We are clumsy, repetitious, passive, and envious of those younger than we are.

Seen through the lens of stereotype, we are doddering along well past our prime and don't deserve to be respected or listened to. Ineffective and incompetent as we are, we are unlikely to have a significant impact on anyone or anything. At this point, we are not to be taken seriously, because we are fading fast and should be put out to pasture. Besides, haven't we had our share by now? Surely we don't deserve any more.

You've heard all the usual thoughtless clichés: *There's no fool like an old fool. You can't teach an old dog new tricks. Their interest in sex is undignified.* And so they push us to the margins of society and relegate us to demeaning positions. They don't see us and are afraid even to look at us, for we are not quite human—a separate and unwelcome category of being.

These age-casting and ageist attitudes are clearly not held by everyone, nor are they projected onto everyone who is older. Some outliers—exceptional seniors with remarkable personality or talent, or who have high status or power and wealth—may be exempt from this stigmatization. But ageism and age-casting are common enough that the vast majority of older people must suffer them in one form or another.

What ageist attitudes and feelings have you taken on? Do you have lowered self-esteem because you are in later life? Or do you reject others for the same reason? By carefully examining our own feelings about aging, we can discover our own preconceptions, misunderstandings, and self-fulfilling prophecies. We can also learn more about the truths and realities of aging that are so different from the prejudices in our society.

How do we come to incorporate these ageist attitudes that are so injurious to our own welfare? Other people and the media inundate us with images and expectations of decrepitude, confusion, and dependency. Both consciously and unconsciously, we accept these images and expectations because they are so pervasive and taken for granted. Eventually, the expectations become embedded in our view of ourselves, and we act in accordance with what is expected or predicted for us. Ageism incorporates just enough reality—we *are* slower and not as strong as we once were—to give it some grounding in fact. But the reality is partial and fragmented, and the vast bulk of ideas about us are gross preconceptions or misconceptions—and, thus, prejudices. For example, we are quite capable of learning new things and remembering them and continuing to learn at a fairly high rate.

A *New York Times* article elaborates on this fact.

THE AGING BRAIN:
The Mind Is Resilient, It's the Body That Fails

Old age's ravages on the human body are inevitable: the eyes dim, the skin sags, the muscles soften. But the common belief that the mind too loses its edge may be just a misperception.

A new set of scientific studies suggests that the brain does not necessarily lose function or reasoning ability as it ages. Actual disease, not age in itself, may underline many or even most cases of feeblemindedness in the elderly, according to the new interpretations.

"Most notions about aging and the brain are based on folklore rather than fact," said Dr. Zaven Khachaturian, a director of research at the National Institute on Aging.

"If you really study aging carefully and look at it in the absence of disease, there is no reason to believe that aging per se leads to decline and loss of cognitive and intellectual activities."

"It is clear that there is a population of old people that escapes in some sense, whose brain function is like that of a younger person," said Dr. Fred Plum of New York Hospital–Cornell Medical Center.[12]

SEEING THROUGH THE LIE

When we see through and discard our own ageism and age-casting, we can begin to see them for what they are: self-serving stereotypes and defenses against the anxieties of people who are afraid to confront their own future aged self.

Although this devaluation of older people is so pervasive in our culture that it seems normal, it is anything but. In many societies around the world, elderly people are not shipped off to nursing homes. They are not

---

12 Gina Kolata, "The Aging Brain: The Mind Is Resilient, It's the Body that Fails," *New York Times,* April 16, 1991, C1.

seen as a burden external to the normal flow of life. Rather, elders are some of the most valued people in their communities for their knowledge, wisdom, and the contributions they have made over their lifetimes and can continue to make.

While we cannot change our society and its treatment of the elderly overnight, we can work toward change, and we can certainly change whatever ageism we have in ourselves that limits us and keeps us from living fully and fulfillingly in later life.

Despite my personal struggles to eliminate these attitudes, the battle is never quite finished. I must constantly be alert to my ageist blind spots. One of the ways I keep alive the struggle against ageist assumptions is to point out to myself and others whenever "old" is associated with feebleness, decrepitude, or other negative qualities.

How can we begin working on ourselves to get rid of our own ageist attitudes? For starters, we can become acquainted with the vast body of research that shows the continuing growth, learning, and developmental potential of people over sixty. We can read about the large number of people at an advanced age who continue to be productive and creative, making important contributions to others and society. We can decondition ourselves by counting our own and our peers' abilities and comparing them with what is expected of us. We can focus on the areas where we can contribute greatly and do our best, disabusing ourselves of the belief that life might be "over" at our age. We can think about fashioning our lives the way we want them to be. In contrast to ageist views, we can consider alternative attitudes and expectations to approach aging with, which help make later life more appealing and challenging and provide a context for viewing it.

Finally, we can adopt some or all of the following attitudes and assumptions about older people and later life: Every human life is precious and can be shaped—at any age—by its possessor into an instrument of beauty, usefulness, caring, creativity, experiential intensity, fuller awareness, and increased humanness. Our life, health, self-esteem, self-worth, and opportunity to derive continuing satisfaction in living are just as important as anyone else's. All of us share a common humanity and have much to contribute to humankind. As long as we live, it is important to keep being who we want to be, and not just what others expect us to be.

We have much to offer in skill, knowledge, wisdom, and perspective. We, more than most, can identify important values, maintain an honorable moral code, understand the human condition, handle our failures and celebrate our successes, deal with others in a sensitive and responsible way, and get in touch with our deeper and more authentic selves.

Let us feel proud and good about our current age and see it as an achievement and a continuation of our special qualities and lives. Let us think of ourselves as a select group to which the price of admission is a minimum of sixty years' accumulated knowledge, caring, and wisdom.

Aging is a day-to-day affair in which each day affords the opportunity to come to terms with an issue and fulfill ourselves in some way and make a contribution to others. Older age has nothing to prove, nothing to win, nothing to compete for, nothing to boast about, no need to excel, no need to be number one, no need to make a fortune or be a big success. We have a diversity of lifestyles, outlooks, attitudes, values, and beliefs. Thus, we are different from each other as well as from the young. Yet we are the same in our basic humanness.

As I aged, I came to see myself as a source and expression of the great chain of being. We are links in the continuity of that chain. We are part of a greater whole. At my age, I hunger to penetrate the mysteries of life. I wonder if they will find me or I will find them. And if I do, what will I know, and what will I do with that knowledge?

We are fortunate to have reached our older age. (Consider the alternative.) Later life is a time for reimagining: discarding old illusions and acquiring new metaphors, hopefully with a little more awareness that they are metaphors.

Some thoughts to live by:

- In older age, expect the worst. If it doesn't come, be grateful.

- In older age, expect the best. If you don't get it, wonder why.

- Old age must be the greatest time of all, for it was left till the end.

- Everyone has a right to be what they were meant to be, that is, to fulfill their potential.

- Old age can be the best time of our life or the worst time of our life. It depends on what we do with it.

As we age, we tend to close our world. The challenge is to keep open, expanding our horizons, our mind, our compassion and empathy, and seek new experiences, open ourselves up to new hopes and new wonders. Later life is a time for celebrating something big or small every day. And it is also a time for grieving on occasions when grief is called for.

By coming to terms with our own ageism, we may learn how to accept ourselves, approve of ourselves, and even love ourselves as aging persons. We may feel that we are a worthy and a worthwhile person, not despite our age but *because* of it—because of who and what we are as an older person. Once we have come to that positive regard for ourselves, it might be easier to challenge age-casting and ageism wherever they appear.

To hell with ageist expectations. Let's turn them on their heads and show them that we can age gloriously and with true grit. If not now, when?

SIX

Issues in Later Life

Later life brings its own set of challenges. In our sixties, seventies, eighties, and nineties, we can expect natural and inevitable declines and dysfunctions. These will vary in intensity and severity in different individuals of different ages. We will have to make a continuing series of adjustments in response to our bodily declines and their ripples and reverberations in our emotional and psychic life. In later life, we may find ourselves facing new emotional issues, or we may try to come to terms with unresolved issues from earlier in life. Some of the issues we face as we grow older are social. They come from our relationships with others or from problems in society—for example, ageism, economic troubles, or fears about personal safety. Others are more personal, such as unfulfilled needs for personal security, satisfying relationships, a strong sense of self, and self-expression. We may also face fears that have become more intense as we grew older, particularly fears of injury, illness, loss, and death and dying. We may also have regrets about how our lives have taken shape so far, and we might wish we had done some things differently. The challenge in later life is to find the most effective and helpful way to deal with our needs, fears, and regrets and then proceed to age well and become the best people we can be.

CHANGE

For most of us, later life brings changes we must adapt to. As we age into later life, many of us have a deep desire to keep our lives the same. Sameness provides familiarity and security. Yet, no matter how much we hope that our lives, our bodies, and our environment remain the same, they inevitably do change. We should ask ourselves how resistant, or how open, we are to change.

As we grow older, many of us tend to close down—continue old habit patterns, become more intransigent in our ways of thinking and doing. We may resist a change in residence, in relationships, in routines. Change, especially major change, sometimes actually brings about distress. For example, the father of a friend of mine became quite upset when he moved to an apartment from the house where he had lived some fifty to sixty years. We are often reluctant to shed old ways of doing things and insist stubbornly on continuing to live in old, established ways. Observing our reactions to change can help us understand how change affects us and can help us prepare for later changes. How do we respond to changes imposed on us without our consent, especially those that are inescapable (e.g., new neighbors with noisy children, or a decline in health)? Similarly, how adaptable are we to changes we initiated but that didn't turn out the way we expected?

We may like or dislike the changes that confront us, put up with them or protest them vociferously. We may vow to resist them or give in and accommodate them. Our reactions to change depend on the magnitude of the change, how much it demands of us, and our capacity and willingness to change. Of course, we are not closed off to all changes. For example, if we were to win a lottery or make a large gain in the stock market, we would accept this change in our fortunes gladly. The criterion for judging change is generally how much anxiety and distress it brings us versus how much joy and satisfaction.

Most of us will behave in older age more or less the way we always behaved. For example, if we were cautious and shy at forty and fifty, we will be that way at seventy and eighty. If we were slow and deliberate at fifty-five, we will likely be that way at seventy-five. Just the same, we as older people can change our habits and our ways if we are motivated and determined to do so and if we become aware of our old patterns and what we might do about them. Do we expect to behave in ways we've become habituated to over many years, to behave mostly as we have before? On the other hand, do we *wish* to change, and do we *believe* that we can change? Do we expect to keep on changing the rest of our lives?

As we age into later life, we may have to make adjustments in our lives to adapt to changes we cannot always control, such as physical decline, financial changes, changing relationships with others, and changes in our identities. We may have to work actively to deal with our changing needs, face our fears, and deal with regrets we may have. If we wish to work passionately and persistently at achieving our goals, we will undoubtedly have to initiate changes in ourselves and our behavior.

UNFULFILLED NEEDS

Our needs, wishes, and desires motivate us. As we come into older age, we are still needy, that is, filled with desires, wishes, impulses, and longings. Although people in later life have the same needs as adults in any other stage of life—and these needs vary quite a bit from one person to the next—there may be some needs that are more relevant to later life because of our physical, social, and psychic state, because of ageism, and simply because many of our years are behind us.

Needs may take different forms and have varying strengths, but they are unmistakably present, seeking fulfillment. A need might be so strong that the body aches for its object, or it can be as weak as a persistent tickle, reminding us that something is absent. If a need remains unfulfilled, it can leave us in a state of vague discomfort or agitation. When this happens, we have a number of alternatives. Of course, we can try to fulfill the need. If this is not possible, we can renounce the quest and try to suppress it. Or we can decide not to fulfill the need, without discounting its urgency or importance. Sometimes, we must endure the pain and anxiety that accompanies important unfulfilled needs. We can also rely on a substitute and hope that will alleviate the need.

The discussion that follows is intended to invite reflection on some of our important unfulfilled needs, and the vehicles for their fulfillment. I hope it stimulates you to examine your needs and helps you become more fully aware of those unmet needs that are still important for you. I also hope it encourages you to find ways and means to meet your unmet needs, put them aside, or come to terms with them so they don't interfere with the goals you have set for yourself in your later life. It's important to confront and deal with unmet needs and our emotional responses to them so that they don't divert us or distress us to the point where it's hard to focus on our objectives. If our needs are mostly fulfilled—or we can at least come to terms with them—we might have the energy, enthusiasm, and inspiration to vigorously pursue our future goals.

I won't try to discuss all the possible needs that might be asking for fulfillment in later life. They are too numerous. Rather, I'll select a few that seem important to me, and hope they will also be relevant for you.

The need for self-preservation and security includes such things as satisfying your physical needs, maintaining physical and emotional safety, taking care of yourself, and being cared for by others.

Where do we find security? Some older people enjoy the security that comes from being financially well-off. For some of us, though, money is always a problem. For others, security comes from being physically healthy and having been in good health for a long time. Even for those of us who are fortunate and have few economic or health problems, we may still need to find emotional security. My work as a therapist and sociologist has helped me identify some suggestions for developing emotional security. We can be aware of what is happening in us, to us, and around us. We can try to know who we are, and feel good about that person, and have important relationships and friendships with people who care about us and wish us well. Family members are important, and we can also have close relationships with friends and associates outside the family. We can seek out people who are there for us and engage us in ways that enhance our self-esteem.

Hold steadfastly to your beliefs, values, and convictions, and have these supported and reinforced by others who respect you and share your values. Belong to groups that share a common purpose with you. If possible, try to increase your status, power, or personal attractiveness so that others treat you with greater respect.

Manage your own life as much as possible, and influence in a positive way the lives of people who are important to you.

There are, of course, other, more specific ways of attaining a measure of personal security—for example, by being successful on a project we've undertaken, or being skilled and knowledgeable in a particular field, craft, or enterprise. I haven't tried to list all the ways that we can make ourselves feel more secure. It is important for each of us to discover the unique personal conditions for increasing our own security, for only then can we think of being adventurous.

Some older people have little trouble meeting their

needs for emotional security. My friend Natalie enjoys a secure life.

She lives with her husband, and her three daughters live nearby. They have a close and loving relationship. As soon as any issue or problem arises, they immediately get together to work it out. Her grandchildren of various ages come to visit frequently. She is securely anchored in her home and in her family context.

Another friend of mine, Joan, has to work harder at forming relationships that will make her a little more secure. Joan lives alone and makes an effort to keep in touch by telephone with as many friends as she can. She does this especially when she is housebound. She also invites a few people at a time to visit her. Her words and demeanor show how grateful she is for their company, and she asks sweetly but imploringly for people to keep in touch. If she hasn't heard from them for a long time, she'll pick up the phone and say she is calling "just to chat." She thus enhances her security by keeping a circle of friends connected to her.

I have found that meditation enhances my sense of emotional security. Some other older people have learned this, too, as described in this article in the *Boston Globe* of February 12, 1990:

TM FOUND BENEFICIAL TO ELDERLY

You know all those Indian yogis, New Age gurus and mind/body afficionados who have been chanting the virtues of meditation for years? Well, they're onto something. A rigorously controlled, albeit small, study has found that meditation not only makes elderly people feel better, but it prolongs their lives.

Specifically, the results of the Harvard University study show that elderly people in nursing homes who learned Transcendental Meditation (TM) were more likely than their peers to still be living three years after the study began. The TM practitioners were also more likely to feel younger at heart, to have sharper mental powers, and to feel better about themselves than nursing home residents who did not meditate or who practiced other techniques to relax.[13]

---

13 Angela Bass, "TM Found Beneficial to Elderly," *Boston Globe*, February 12, 1990, 33.

The need for validation involves accepting myself and being accepted, admired, and respected by others. When I'm being validated, I get the kind of attention I want, and I am positively regarded by those people who are important to me. I am recognized by others as a member of the human community. It is important to feel esteemed by others—seen as worthy and worthwhile—as this in turn contributes to my own self-esteem. It can be painful and isolating when we don't receive validation from other people.

The need for relatedness involves being needed by others, belonging to groups that we identify with and feel part of, and being able to trust others and be trusted by them. An important aspect of this need, which I will discuss more fully in chapter seven, is the need for intimacy with friends, family members, and others we feel a strong bond with. If our need for relatedness is unfulfilled, we can feel isolated and lonely. But when our needs for relatedness are met, we feel secure and connected to other people; we feel part of a community.

If you cannot fulfill your unmet needs after all your efforts to do so, you could try to live with them as best you can by pushing them into the background and leaving them there as distant phenomena that don't intrude on your day-to-day awareness too often. Either way, try to accept what is, so that you're at peace with your unmet needs and with yourself.

PERSISTENT FEARS

What does it mean to be afraid? In broad terms, it means to anticipate that something dreadful, unwanted, or injurious might happen. Maybe something bad has happened before and we believe it will happen again. Fear is often the mirror image of a need. For example, our need for self-preservation is the other side of our fear of physical injury.

Fears may be large or small, ranging from panic or terror to mild apprehension, enduring or short-lived, conscious or unconscious, keenly felt or vaguely experienced. Some fears are obvious; others less so. Some endure and others dissipate easily. Some overwhelm us and may result in panic, while others are easily handled. Some fears are realistic; others are fantasies manufactured in our minds. Fears may range from a generalized existential insecurity in which the world is a frightening place, to commonplace fears such as that of crossing a street in heavy traffic or forgetting the name of a person we just met. Thus, our fears have different intensities, durations, and directions, and we have different reactions and ways of handling them. These may range from avoidance and flight to confrontation and resolution. The more unresolved and persistent fear-evoking situations we have encountered, the higher the probability that we might become afraid of fear itself.

Our task is to differentiate those fears that are imagined from those that are based on real and present dangers. We also need to learn how to contain, put aside, or transcend our real fears in the interest of our greater comfort.

As we age, we may be and feel more vulnerable: to illness, to deterioration of our bodies, to less efficient functioning, to reduced energy, to accidents, to wearing down, to slower recovery from illness. We might become more fearful of physical injury. Some of the fears we face in later life have always been with us and are fears that many younger people share. Other fears are newly acquired. As we grow older, these can intensify.

Mary, an older friend of mine, says, "I'm so afraid to go out at night. If I do, and this is rare, I'm always with someone. I don't walk anywhere, but ride where I'm going."

Some of the fears we face as we grow older are particular to later life and come as a surprise. For example, I had always considered myself quite agile on my feet. In my seventy-first year, I was walking on the street when a small garbage can rolled in my direction. I wanted to avoid getting hit, so I jumped and swerved, expecting to easily miss it and land on my feet. I did miss the can but landed on the sidewalk on my shoulder, unhurt but shaken. I then understood that these kinds of maneuvers are no longer possible for me. I will have to be more careful in how I try to avoid obstructions. Thus, I became fearful about my vulnerability because I no longer saw myself as the "artful dodger," and I felt that I was now much more susceptible to things that would suddenly block my path and cause me to fall.

In addition to the fears around our bodies, we may have other fears, of failure, risk, or the unknown and unfamiliar. These and other fears can be disruptive forces in our lives, using up our time and energy, immobilizing us, inhibiting us, and preventing us from pursuing our goals.

FEAR OF DEATH AND DYING

I find myself in a struggle with fear of death. The end of everything is a terrifying prospect that I resist with all my heart. But then I know that I should work at accepting death as a natural and inevitable completion to my life. Thus, the question is how to balance my feelings and my rationality. I know I shall die, and I wish

I could accept it more easily. Yet I resist and resent the awareness, the fear, and the very fact of death itself. But I also want to learn how to come to terms with death so that I am unafraid and finally can depart calmly, peacefully, and contentedly. I want to appreciate the fact that death is an ever-present possibility, but not become preoccupied or immobilized by it. I want to be undeterred by the prospect of death so that I can live fully. Perhaps, the resolution to wish for is to welcome death when I am very old, very tired, with little life energy and very ready to go, having led a fulfilled life.

To some extent, most of us fear the fact that we will die eventually. We are reluctant to confront this inevitable reality. What, specifically, do we fear? We fear the possible pain and suffering in the process of dying, and the circumstances we might die under, especially if we were to linger on in an unconscious or vegetative state. We dread the anguish that we might experience during our final days. We are pained because of the suffering and distress our death will cause others. We fear the end of experiencing, the loss of ego, the loss of our relationships—the loss of everything we hold dear. We dread the idea of no longer being able to enjoy and respond to the world. We resist the realization that we will have to sever our attachments and connections with those we hold dear. We fear the end of desire, interest, activity, and involvement. We dread feelings of annihilation, nonexistence, and a descent into nothingness. And we shiver at the thought of embarking on an unknown journey with an unknown destination, completely alone. Where, if anywhere, are we going?

The conception of being no more when we have always been is difficult to absorb. Awareness of our mortality in our later years takes on a certain poignancy that was not there before. Dying becomes more than a concept or an idea. It becomes more real. As we age in later life and each day brings us closer to the end of our lives, our fear may grow while our days get shorter.

Max Lerner, in his book *Wrestling with the Angel*, has this to say about death and later life:

> *Aging is a stage of life, death a finality. The fear of death is the fear of the unknown as well as the terminal. The fear of aging is the fear of the all too well known. Both prod us into activity. Along with the maladies in its wake, aging forms our early warning system of the approach of death. The fear of death spurs us to invent energies and busyness that will mask its terror from us. The fear of aging— limiting the compass of our lives, diminishing the time that still remains for fruitful functioning— spurs us to fall back and reinvent ourselves, to savor more fully the life that remains. This means to*

*reimagine who and where we are, what we want
of the rest of our lives, what we can whittle away
as inessential, what becomes central.*[14]

Facing our mortality can help us both to prepare for dying and to enjoy life more fully. How shall we prepare for death? What difference can our attitudes and emotional sets make? Can we have any control over feelings and thoughts about dying? What would be a proper, dignified, peaceful, or good way to approach our death and dying? The way we deal with our fear of death and dying greatly influences how we age. Some of us dread death. Some of us just forget about it and go on living. We can try to face death boldly and forthrightly until our fear has lost its power to stifle us. Some of us "rage, rage against the dying of the light" as Dylan Thomas urged; others accept the idea of death calmly, with the understanding that it is an inevitable part of the natural life process. These people look upon death in a matter-of-fact way, taking for granted that it will happen to them. Thus, they live from day to day without the fear of death intruding into their lives.

---

14 Max Lerner, *Wrestling with the Angel: A Memoir of My Triumph over Illness.* New York: Simon & Schuster, 1990.

Here is how my friend David feels about it:

I feel satisfied with my life and I shuffle off, not gladly, not unregretfully, but not angrily. I don't shake my fists saying, "Why are you taking me?" I'm seventeen years beyond seventy. I've had a full life until recently, when I had my accident. People have played a major role in my life, and that has always been my joy. At my age, to have a love affair with a woman for the past year, to have it come about so naturally and spontaneously—it's a great way to end your life. The probabilities, at eighty-seven, of an extended future are rather limited. Yet I'm planning to be here until 1999. I want to be here for the dinner at Loch Ober's on December 31, 1999. My brother and I have promised each other a dinner at that time. I've worked out the scenario for my dying. I want to die with my boots on—to drop off the platform after my last lecture. No suffering! Just stop! Go fast! Don't linger!

A *Boston Globe* article from August 10, 1990, tells about B. F. Skinner, the famous behavioral psychologist, at age eighty-six:

ZEAL FOR LIFE UNTO END

B. F. Skinner, world-renowned behavioral psychologist, is facing death from leukemia with the same intellectual zeal that has marked his long and productive career . . . "I'm not afraid to go," he said . . . Though Skinner's body is frail, his mind remains strong and agile . . . He has faced [his critics] as matter-of-factly as he is facing death . . . He is not arguing with death, either, but is deeply saddened for his family . . . "You can't help hurting people when you die . . . I haven't the slightest bit of worry or anxiety about it. I'm not religious, so I don't have to worry about punishment after death."[15]

How might we approach the unavoidable fact of our mortality?

We can think about the deaths of others, and confront the idea of our own death, so that we appreciate and cherish life more. We can talk about our fears and

---

15 Gloria Negri, "Zeal for Life unto End: Behaviorist B.F. Skinner Facing Up to Death," *Boston Globe,* August 10, 1990. 1.

the way we think about death with our friends or families. Some of us find comfort in putting ourselves "in the hands of God." Some of us view our death with objectivity and detachment, all the while accepting its reality. Others of us see death not as a termination but as a passage to another place. Some of us go to therapy or join a support group to help face our fear of death and dying. All these suggestions can help us find peace, and our hope is to be able to say, "I've led a good life, a full life, a useful life, and I'm ready to go."

If we don't come to terms with our fear of death, it will undoubtedly interfere with our living fully—for example, in the fear of taking risks and in the fear of committing ourselves fully to another person, and in restricting our desire and our freedom of movement and exploration. For many of us, the fear of death and dying is the ultimate fear. But if we can make some inroads into that fear, we might be able to reduce or eliminate many other fears. If we did not fear death, how much less frightening other fears would be!

FEAR OF ILLNESS, INJURY, DISABILITY, PAIN AND SUFFERING

Associated with the fear of death and dying is the fear of physical injury, illness, disability, and pain and suffering. For example, a fall, an auto collision, or a friend's accident may remind us that the bases for these fears are real and that we are especially vulnerable to physical injury. Fear of physical attack keeps many people, especially women, in their houses at night, and this fear may become even more pronounced in later life. For many elders, riding a subway or walking in the street late at night stirs up apprehension and watchfulness to minimize the danger.

All kinds of fantasies come with fear of illness. We fear being handicapped or disabled; we fear being under the control and authority of others (in and out of the hospital); we fear that we will suffer unbearable pain; we fear that others will pity us. We fear that we will be depressed, that we will become diminished and incomplete people. We fear that we will be too dependent on others, that we will feel childlike and humiliated. We fear that the illness may result in our death. These fears might be highly exaggerated and mostly fantasy, or based on experience and reality.

A severe illness can reduce us emotionally and bring us down psychologically, assault our self-esteem and our self-image, erode our self-confidence, and exclude us from the stream of life. No wonder illness looms large as a dominant fear among older people! We are more susceptible and vulnerable to it. It is harder for us to fight illness, and we take longer to recover than younger people do.

With a severe illness, there is the danger that we will become self-centered and preoccupied with our illness or disability—thinking about it constantly, talking about it incessantly to anyone who will listen, and making it the dominant focus of our lives. This can make us unpopular with others, compounding our worries and feelings of isolation.

In one of my groups for seniors, all one of the members could talk about was his illness: his worries about it, his fear that it would persist, that he didn't know what to do about it, that it made him so anxious he couldn't sleep at night. He went on and on in this way for the entire session. It was impossible to stop him or divert him, and he succeeded in turning the group against him.

Of course, some older people take their illness in stride: trying to cure it, accommodating themselves to it, living with it, or accepting it without letting it dominate their lives. Illness, strangely, can also have a positive side. It can help us put our lives in perspective, because illness often forces us to take stock of our lives and decide what we really care about or believe to be important.

Max Lerner again tells about the perspective gained with illness:

> *To cope with a life-threatening illness at any time, and succeed in overcoming it, has to be in itself a life-changing experience. To be close to death*

"powerfully concentrates a (person)," as Dr. Johnson put it. When the illness comes late in life, it adds a touch at once of pathos and piquancy. The pathos is that so few years remain for living with the renewed depth you have achieved. The piquancy is that you are spurred even more to rethink life, to reinvent yourself, to ask the embracing question: What shall I do with the rest of my life?[16]

At some point in my seventy-fourth year, I was suddenly invaded by a severe fatigue, labeled a "malaise" by my physician. The term masked the fact that neither he nor the specialist I was referred to could diagnose the disease. Meanwhile, the disease sapped my energy. On day one, I could scarcely get out of bed. All my ordinary activities stopped, and I felt as if I was between sleeping and waking. Fantasy and reality were all confused, and I was too tired to sort them out. My mind was hazy, and I couldn't make fine distinctions. I felt disconnected and removed from everything. Every move took great effort and became an occasion for near exhaustion. I had to lie down frequently and, when walking, move slowly with small steps and for short

---

16 Max Lerner, *Wrestling with the Angel: A Memoir of My Triumph over Illness* (New York: Simon & Schuster, 1990), 157-158.

distances. I suffered greatly from an inability to control the extent and force of my movements.

Day by day, the illness diminished and my energy returned, so that I could undertake some ordinary tasks. My mind awakened after a few days, and after a week I was almost back to normal. But I was left with the dread that the illness might return. And indeed it did, a few months later, in a less severe form. Thus, my fear was reinforced. As the malaise returned on a cycle of every six weeks (though in a less severe form), I became less frightened of it. Because it was familiar and less incapacitating, I could cope with it and not let it interfere in my daily routine. It eventually disappeared, and after a few months I completely forgot about it and no longer dreaded its possible return.

Fear of pain and suffering is a fear, whether conscious or unconscious, shared by most everyone I know. We all want to avoid pain and suffering and to relieve them when they occur. Pain, however, is not avoidable throughout a lifetime. From one point of view, physical pain has a positive function: it signals that something has gone wrong or that a dysfunction of the body has occurred and we had better pay attention. Physical pain can be controlled or even eliminated by drugs, sleep, and sedation, but unless you address the *source* of the pain, it will be there when you wake up or the drug wears off.

Pain is often equated with suffering, yet they are quite different. We can suffer from the death of a loved one, a psychic injury, or a separation in a relationship and not have the same experience as when we break a leg, the dentist hits a nerve, or we have a severe illness. The thing that binds pain and suffering together is the intense discomfort and the feeling that we will not be able to "stand it," that we might die of it.

Many people have told me that they don't fear death as much as they fear the pain and suffering that might come in the process of dying. It is the experience of pain and suffering that drives them to distraction, to seek drugs, painkillers, or any substance that will dull the pain and suffering. And it is both the experience of pain and suffering and the anticipation of them that generates fear.

FEAR OF LOSSES AND OTHER TRAGEDIES

When we lose a child, a spouse, parent, or other intimate, powerful emotions are evoked. Sometimes we witness another person's tragedy and feel sorrow, fearing that "it might happen to me." A story in the *New York Times* describes a woman's painful reaction to her grandmother's aging.

As my grandmother has worsened, so too has my response to her. My mother implores me to be decent and stay in touch, and I launch into all the reasons why I don't. But my excuses sound shallow and glib, even to myself. The truth is that my grandmother terrifies me. I have in my mind a pastel confection of the perfect old woman. She is wise and dignified, at peace with herself and quietly proud of the life she has forged . . . Of course, there are many things my fantasy doyenne is not. She's not strapped for money. Her joints don't ache, her breath doesn't rattle. She isn't losing her memory, her reason, her eyesight. Above all, she is not the old woman I know best.

I love my grandmother. She still has her good hours, when her mind is quick and clear. Inevitably, though, her mad despair bursts to the surface again. She discovers a new reason to weep, blame and backstab, and I discover a new excuse for staying away.

I want to age magnificently . . . I want to be better in half a century than I am at 31, but I doubt that I will. When I look at my

> grandmother, fragile, frightened, unhappy,
> wanting to die but clinging desperately to life,
> I see myself—and I cannot stand the sight.[17]

I had a colleague, Joseph, who one day, while driving me home, asked me if I thought there was any loss worse than a child losing a parent at an early age. When I said I didn't think so, since I had lost my own mother at age eight, he replied, "A worse loss is for a parent to lose a child at any age." He had lost a son at nineteen, in an automobile accident a few years ago. He had grieved long and intensely and had come to terms with the loss, mostly. He felt it was God's way of teaching him that life is fragile, not to waste it, and to live as fully as you can in doing the most that you can for others.

Anyone who has experienced such a tragic loss knows the profoundly disturbing and traumatic effect that it can have. As a consequence, we may fear that with the loss of another intimate, the world will come to an end, that we could not go on living, that we would never be able to smile again, or that life would hold no

---

17 Natalie Angier, "Hers; A Granddaughter's Fear," *New York Times,* May 8, 1989, 22

meaning. The previous tragedy may have had such a powerful effect that it was difficult to get a perspective on what was happening at the time.

The older we get, the more of these losses we will have to suffer: another relative or another friend dies; another companion has to go to a nursing home. It might seem that every time we turn around, someone close to us is departing. We might begin to fear that the losses will be endless, going on and on until we ourselves are the ones who are the object of someone else's loss.

FEAR OF LOSING OUR "SELF"

As we age, we may come to believe that we have "lost" our former self as a consequence of the aging process. We may fear that as we continue to age, we may completely lose ourselves. We might fear that the "self" we once were is slowly or rapidly changing into someone else. We may fear that we won't recognize ourselves as we get older. And we may be concerned that if we become very different, we will be unrecognizable to others in the future.

We might experience a loss of "self" through a decline in physical functioning, because we have difficulty managing our lives or coping with changes in personality, or from memory failure and diminution of mental activity. Aging is a frightening prospect if we expect that in later life, loss or deterioration of the self is an inevitable accompaniment to deterioration of the body. It is important to raise questions about the myth that aging means losing our identity along with some of our physical capacity. There is no necessary correlation between the two. We can have an agile mind even if we have a fragile body. We should remember to affirm to ourselves that the body is only one aspect of our self and not our total self.

Ageism, both that of other people and our own internalized ageism, can also make us feel a loss of identity and make us wonder if we have an identifiable presence. We fear a "loss of self" when others with ageist beliefs treat us as inconsequential nobodies.

If we believe that we have been diminished as we've grown older, and as a consequence are inadequate or unacceptable, we may cling to remnants or images of our former selves. We might experience a loss of self when we can no longer feel connected to our earlier self. Our experience of our changing self, and the fears we have about it, might be better handled if we can make a continuing connection between our previous and current selves, if we can integrate the self we are now with the selves we once were.

FEARS OF DEPENDENCY AND DECLINE

We often fear losing control when we cannot manage our affairs. When this happens, we may feel that we are no longer the undisputed "captain of our ship," the one in charge of our journey through life. Aging in later life can at times be a distressing experience. We might become afraid of losing control over our emotions when we burst into tears unexpectedly, are quick to anger, or are easily upset. We may fear surrendering control to others around us when people tell us what to do, or put us in places we don't want to be (such as assisted living). We might fear losing control over our finances if we can no longer take care of them or manage them competently. We might fear losing control over our thoughts and mind, so that we are no longer coherent and no longer seen as mentally competent. Finally, we may fear that we will become diminished enough to jeopardize our very survival.

The basic issue here is whether we have cause to believe that the power to direct our lives has flowed out of our hands. Our fear of losing control might generate desperate attempts to retain control. Or, despairing, we surrender to control by others. Or we may be motivated to find ways of exerting such control over our lives, if that is possible.

Sometimes, experiences in our earlier lives may make dependence and loss of control especially frightening. Below is an excerpt from a story in the *Washington Post*, about a famous psychologist, Bruno Bettelheim, who was a concentration camp survivor. It tells about his fear of loss of control, his fear of decline and dependence, and his decision to end his life.

> [O]n the night of March 12, Bettelheim killed himself at the Charter House retirement home in Silver Spring . . . When Los Angeles analyst Rudolph Ekstein first learned about his old friend's suicide, he wondered if Bettelheim were thinking thoughts like these: "I have to live now in a retirement home, and it will be like the freedom lost when I was in the concentration camp. Why do I have to survive? What am I waiting for? I want to at least have control," . . .
>
> "It was so clear that he was depressed," says historian Joan Challinor, who talked with him for 45 minutes at a dinner. "He said he now knew that he should have gone to Israel, because there the kibbutzes knew how to create a situation in which old people could be useful."[18]

Most of us can expect to deal with some decline in our mental capacities as we age into later life. We may

---

18 David Streitfeld, "For Bruno Bettelheim, a Place to Die," *Washington Post*, April 24, 1990, C1.

become disoriented and find ourselves having trouble with simple things that we wouldn't have given a second thought in earlier life. Many of us have had some experiences of disorientation and may now have some fear of its recurrence. We may have had the experience of suddenly not knowing where we are, of being mixed up, unfocused, or fuzzy, even if only for a few brief moments. Sometimes, we forget what we need to know in order to get where we're going, or we forget what we just started to do. We might forget something we really want to remember or something we used to know well—for example, when we see people we've known for a long time and I don't recognize them. Sometimes, memories and images of situations lose their sharpness and appear dimmer than they were before. These signs and others might even frighten us into believing we are losing our mind. But Ken Dychtwald reassures us in his book *Age Wave*, "Study after scientific study has shown that [older] people who stay active and intellectually challenged not only maintain their mental alertness but also live longer."[19]

I have experienced disorientation from time to time, and I see it not as evidence of disease, but as a

---

19 Ken Dychtwald, *Age Wave: How the Most Important Trend of Our Time Will Change Your Future* (New York: Bantam, 1990).

normal part of getting older. To be afraid of being disoriented raises our anxiety and contributes to the very disorientation we fear. Accepting occasional disorientation can make it easier to come to terms with it when it occurs. Putting our experiences of disorientation in perspective can help make them seem less frightening. To orient ourselves to our disorientation, we should ask ourselves how long the confusion persists, how often it occurs, how disruptive it is in our daily functioning, and what we can do to prevent, compensate for, or adjust to it.

Other occasions for fearing a loss of control arise when we have to restrict our activities. The further we progress into older life, the more restricted our activities ordinarily become. We may be restricted from going on long trips away from home because of our physical condition. If we have arthritis, we may be restricted in our physical movements. Because of other disabilities or sheer eyestrain, we may not be able to read easily or as much as we did before. With a reduced energy level, we may not be able to socialize as much as we used to. The experience of one or more restrictions, and our fear of their continued expansion into more areas of our life, may make us sad, depressed, angry, or frustrated. Can we learn to overcome or diminish some of our restrictions? Or compensate for them? If we can't overcome or diminish them, can we accept them with grace and dignity and come to terms with them?

FEAR OF THE UNKNOWN AND THE UNFAMILIAR

Here I will discuss just one of the consequences of fear of the unknown: the fear of taking risks. When we risk, we enter the unknown. This may arouse fear or anxiety, which must be contained if the risk is to be undertaken. We might be afraid to start new projects, meet new people, visit new places, break old habits, change our physical environment, or question long-held points of view. Underlying all these fears of risk-taking may be the fear of failure. We may fear that something terrible will happen, that we will be made uncomfortable, that we will lose the security that comes with familiarity, or that we will become lost or confused. We may fear that taking the risk will be too difficult, that "it isn't worth it," that risk-taking is dangerous and subjects us to the possibility of injury. We may avoid risks because caution has been advantageous in the past. We can become concerned that things will grow unstable in the risk-taking and that we will be worse off after taking the risk than we were before.

Sometimes, as we grow older, we fear taking small risks that would not have given us a moment's pause in earlier life. If we have experienced a decline in our physical or mental powers, fear of taking these small risks may be quite realistic and appropriate.

In later life, we may fear taking bigger risks as well. Our fears may keep us from new experiences that we might enjoy very much. Fear of risk-taking is often prudent and realistic, and caution can save us all a lot of heartache. If we take caution too far, however, and exaggerate the risk in trying new things, we might miss out on wonderful experiences. By putting risk in perspective, we may be able to face reasonable risks with courage and enjoy our later lives as fully as possible.

FEAR OF REJECTION AND ABANDONMENT

Many elders fear that we will be "left"—rejected or abandoned by people who used to care about us, such as our spouses, children, and long-term friends. Abandonment might come about because our relationships with intimates have become problematic due to a severe disagreement over an important issue, or simply because we have changed as we've grown older, acquiring new attitudes, values, and beliefs. Old quarrels and difficulties can reemerge in later life. As we age, we may no longer be seen as desirable or worthwhile. Others may see us as irascible, crotchety, spiteful, or complaining.

Dependency can also bring up our fears of

abandonment. We fear that our children will get tired of looking after us, or a new set of interests will occupy them so that they have no time for us. Our family may think that the demands we make are excessive and burdensome. They may even feel that we don't care about them, since the aging process places more demands on their time and energy.

Rejection may take the form of less frequent visits, telephone calls, or letters, or other signs of not wanting much contact. In extreme instances, intimates might sever contact with us completely. This can be devastating, especially in a child-parent relationship. If, despite entreaties and attempts to communicate, nothing works and there is no reciprocity, we may have to face the fact that the rejection is complete and final. With that clarity may come a rush of feelings: guilt, bitterness, disappointment, anger. We may have feelings of betrayal, thoughts of *how much I've done for them* and *how much I've sacrificed*. We may fall into a state of mourning for some time and ask ourselves, *How can I live with this?*

Other feelings may arise: fears of having no one to care for us when we really need them, or not feeling worthwhile and adequate because, somehow or other, we might be responsible for the rejection and the abandonment. The pain and the hurt may manifest in a reluctance to form new and close relationships. But there may come a time when the abandonment no longer dominates our feelings, and we put it to rest and accept that we may not see our loved ones again. We come to terms with the abandonment but may still feel a dull ache that comes intermittently to remind us of our loss.

Alice had worked as a psychotherapist well into her eighty-fifth year. Approaching eighty-six, she began to fail somewhat, becoming forgetful and confused at times. Because she had earned enough over forty years of practice, she could maintain her household and profession with a number of helpers. She had a secretary, a handyman, part-time household help, and a live-in student, who all enabled her to live at home and carry on her life in much the same way she had in the past. But it was expensive. Because she recognized that she could not easily handle her finances, she signed over the power of attorney to her son John. John saw his inheritance disappearing if these large yearly expenditures should continue and urged Alice to move to a nursing home. Alice agreed to the transfer because John promised that she would be able to continue her therapeutic work there. This promise was never kept, and as soon as Alice moved in she was put under the same restrictive conditions as other residents in the nursing home. John had also promised Alice that she would not have to stay if she didn't like it. As soon as she moved in, it became apparent to her that this was not the place for her. Despite her pleas and complaints, John insisted that she stay in the nursing home, which she did. And there she died a few months after her admission.

FEAR OF ECONOMIC DEPRIVATION

Some of us fear that we will suffer economic deprivation, and many of us are actually in difficult economic straits. Thus, the fear may be realistic, or it may be an exaggeration of our actual situation. But I have found that many people in later life, whatever their income, fear that they might not have enough money to do the things they want to do, or to stay in the home they want to keep.

The fear of physical deprivation may haunt our thoughts and fantasies, especially if we have come from a poverty-stricken childhood. Old memories of hunger, lack of decent housing, or insufficient clothing are easily evoked. Thus, even though our financial situation is much better now, a recession or drop in income may fuel the fear of being unable to acquire the basic necessities. Apprehension and even dread may become a powerful source of agitation and concern even though deprivation is not realistic or imminent. For many of us, these fears are precipitated by memories of the Great Depression and the misery and suffering we endured and observed others undergoing.

A *Boston Globe* article has the heading "Burdens of Growing Older Seen Behind Rise in Suicides."

BURDENS OF GROWING OLDER SEEN BEHIND RISE IN SUICIDES

So distraught was a retired schoolteacher over his inability to care for his ailing wife properly that he wrote this note shortly before his 69th birthday: "I can no longer provide for the two of us on my meager Social Security. At least, through my death, you can live on the insurance money. Please destroy this note so you can collect the full insurance benefits. I love you."

. . . Overwhelmed by loneliness, loss of income, the death of a spouse or a debilitating illness, the nation's elders take their own lives more often than any other age group.[20]

---

20 Diane E. Lewis, "Burdens of Growing Older Seen Behind Rise in Suicides," *Boston Globe*, November 28, 1988, 1-10.

DEALING WITH OUR FEARS

What can we do about our fears? We can try to ignore them and act as if they didn't exist. We can behave as if they were impossible to deal with, and flee from them in whatever way we can. We can do nothing about them and hope they disappear. Unfortunately, our fears may remain with us and make it difficult to live our lives fully. We may be better off to confront our fears, endure them, or resist them as long as we can. Or we can try to transform our fears into a source of strength.

We can also try to put our fears in perspective. We can seek out information about the risks we take in our lives. We can rely on the wisdom we have gained from life so far, and we can rest assured that we must be very strong because we have survived so much for so long. We can talk with others about fears, and perhaps they can offer clarification about how realistic our fears are.

Finally, we might try to achieve genuine acceptance of our fears by making friends with them. We might intensely dislike having fears, but perhaps we can suspend our negative feeling and try not to reject, deny, or resist a particular fear. If we can relate to fear as just another aspect of our being, if we can be patient with ourselves when we are afraid, our fears may diminish or disappear. And if they don't, then we might try to figure out how to live with fear and, despite its presence in our lives, resolve to pursue our goals and live life fully.

REGRETS AND THE REGRETTED

It would be surprising indeed if, during a long life, there weren't at least some events, relationships, and paths taken that we now regret. Our regrets can be persistent reminders of troublesome issues that we still must deal with, or they can be occasional reminders of events in our personal history we are unhappy about. It might be beneficial to identify our regrets—to ask ourselves in retrospect, *How important are these regrets to me now? How deeply do I feel about them? And what, if anything, do I want to do about them?*

Feelings of bitterness, resentment, or depression that accompany regrets may interfere with our becoming the best person we can be. Persistent remorse about a particular situation or relationship may preoccupy us and make it difficult to focus on other matters. Remorse can immobilize us and prevent us from taking actions that involve any degree of risk or uncertainty. Dwelling on regrets about what went wrong might make us passive and hesitant.

How often have we had these thoughts? *If I could only start all over again, I could avoid all the mistakes I made,* or

I could use my accumulated knowledge and understanding to take different paths and have a much better life. If that hadn't happened, how different my life would have been! Do we say to ourselves, *I didn't lead my life right?* If we can put our regrets aside or come to terms with them, we can enjoy the years we have ahead of us more fully.

Here are some of the things that many older people regret. Think about which of these speak to you or have been part of your life.

LOSSES

We regret the death of a loved one, especially if it came before their time, because it was so devastating to us to face many years of life without that special person. And we regret the loss of health and energy. We feel that we've grown old too soon and lost the self we once were.

My decision to travel while I was sick may have made me sicker. I regret having gone to China when I had bronchitis. My asthma was caused by the pollution in Shanghai.

We regret the loss of relationships with other people—because we abandoned them or they abandoned us, or because we never resolved conflicts in the relationship.

We feel regret over the loss of an important part of our identity, such as a job or an important interest.

UNRESOLVED DIFFICULTIES WITH OTHERS

Many of us have contributed to the disruption or damage of relationships, promised things we never delivered, harbored grudges and resentments (sometimes over decades), and failed to work through conflicts and disagreements.

Michael, a friend of mine, regrets severing an important friendship: "I had a long and warm relationship with a couple. At one point, my parents were killed in an automobile accident. They were there when my brother called to tell me the bad news. They beat a hasty retreat and I never heard from them during my period of mourning. I was so hurt and angry. They later tried to resume the relationship. I turned them away."

OUR DEFICIENCIES AND INADEQUACIES

We regret our own shortcomings—those aspects of our personalities that are undeveloped or unexpressed. We bemoan our continuing difficulties in making and keeping relationships, and the times when we violated our own code of conduct and compromised our integrity. We look back with shame on the things we did out of spite or meanness (such as not lending money to a friend who was in desperate need, even though we could afford it, to get back at them for some real or imagined slight). And we cringe at all the times we should have spoken out but kept quiet, and the times we spoke but shouldn't have.

OUR INJURIES—THOSE RECEIVED AND THOSE GIVEN

We wish we had done a better job with our children and had been more involved with our family. And we wish we'd tried harder to have a better relationship with our spouse.

We regret all the psychic injuries we've inflicted on others, and all the envy and jealousy we felt toward those who had the things and relationships that we would have liked to have.

We feel the sting long after having been fooled or betrayed by another, including the occasions when we were physically or emotionally injured. And we regret the injuries born of accidents that caused much pain and suffering, diverting our career or interrupting our personal life.

OUR FAILURES AND MISTAKES

We may regret having done work that came to nothing.

Frank, a colleague, once told me, "How I regret the amount of time and effort I spent on this book. I kept writing and rewriting it, modifying it for the last twenty years. But it never could come out right. I spent these years on it all for naught. It held me back in so many ways—I felt I couldn't start on another project until I finished this one. And I never could get this one finished, so I finally dropped it and was able to start on new things."

My friend Roger, a sixty-year-old retired executive, talks of a common regret. He was out of town a lot and worked late at night in his earlier life. "How I regret not having spent time with my children," he told me. "They are all grown now, and I hardly know them. I missed the best years of their lives, and I can never recapture that. And I feel a certain resentment from them, and a lack of closeness."

We may regret never finishing projects we started. Or not carrying out the plans we devised or honoring commitments we made.

We may rue our lack of success in education, career, or the social sphere. For example, we "didn't make it big" or never achieved the social status or acquired the material possessions we wanted. Maybe we feel we should have worked harder or applied ourselves to realize more of our potential. Or we regret foolish or risky things we did that endangered others or ourselves.

DISAPPOINTMENTS AND MISSED OPPORTUNITIES

Many of us have faced unfulfilled aspirations. We may still feel the pain of an unrequited love. Sara, a friend, once told me, "I regret not having married a man who asked me to be his wife. I've ended up alone, with no one to love and no one to love me."

Some of us lament missing out on adventures and new experiences that appealed to us. Or not choosing a career that was close to our hearts, or not learning the things we wanted to learn. Alan, a friend of many years, tells me, "All these years, I worked at this job that I hated. It paid pretty well, and I needed the money. I had a wife, two kids, a house, and wanted to live a comfortable middle-class life. How often I wished I could leave my job and do what was closest to my heart: to become a teacher of small children. It would have been impossible to make the transition, and even if I could, the pay would have been so much less. But somewhere, deep inside me, I regret that I never followed my heart's path."

The emotional charge in a regret may still be deep and all-pervasive, or weak and occasional. We may still feel it as an emotional sting, a dull pain, or merely a wistful memory. And regrets may come with other feelings: shame, resentment, bitterness, or anxiety. Or they may produce sadness or a wish for another chance. Remembering may bring up incidents that were involved in the original experience and that now occasion the regret. Or we can feel distance and detachment from the event that we regret. Whatever the complex of emotions associated with the regret, and the nature of what is regretted, we may wish to explore ways of coming to terms with our regrets, and try out different ways of putting to rest the gnawing distress that might accompany them.

In reviewing your regrets and their associated feelings, can you stand off and look at them as not necessarily a fixed part of your emotional landscape? Or can you project a vision or fantasy of how your life could have been different if . . . Or you can wonder, *What if I had done so and so?* Or you can daydream about what could have been, and all that you've missed. Or you can think, *That was then and this is now. It's past and not important to me anymore.*

You can use your regrets as a vehicle for coming to terms with some things that have happened in the past that you feel sorry about and wish had not occurred. Or you can use your regrets as an occasion to feel sorry for yourself, punish yourself, bemoan your fate, and rail against your misfortunes or faithless friends. Or you may look at the regretted event from your current perspective and ask yourself what you learned from it. Can you derive some wisdom from the pain? You can ask yourself how the thing you regret contributed to the good, useful, and valuable things you did later and how, as a consequence, your character developed in a positive way. You may be able to see the regrettable situation, which appeared as a failure in the past, as later having contributed to beneficial accomplishments on your part and to your ability to avoid other similar situations.

I have found it quite helpful to acknowledge and accept that I was different then from who I am now but that nevertheless, "I" was the one involved. The more I resisted accepting regretted events and situations I had initiated or had been the principal actor in—the more I resisted their being part of my past—the more pain and regret I felt, the longer that pain persisted, and the more unresolved I felt. But as I permitted myself to be remorseful, I became more accepting of past failures, mistakes, and unacceptable actions. "Accepting" did not mean being happy or pleased with what happened, or that I didn't wish that things had happened differently. Rather, as I admitted them into myself as my own doings, my experiences, I could then take them in and *let them be*, rather than try to avoid or deny them. Before I could deal with some regretted events in my life in this way, I needed to let myself grieve about them. I suggest that you, too, grieve, in ways that are appropriate for you, over the events that you regret most deeply.

It is important that you come to terms with your regrets and situations and with the people you have the regret about. If it hangs heavily on you, keeps you preoccupied with the past, or evokes continual feelings of shame or guilt and keeps you mired in resentment, you may not have the energy or even the desire to seek out ways of becoming the best person you can be.

ACCEPTING YOUR AGING (OR NOT)

The issue is this: How much acceptance or denial, avoidance, or rejection of your aging are you engaged in?

There are many ways of accepting your aging, depending on how far you want to take it. You might accept your aging one day, deny it the next, and completely ignore it on another. You might accept one part of yourself as having aged (e.g., you don't move with the same speed and ease you once had) and reject another part (for example, the decline in mental acuity). Or you might see yourself as having improved rather than declined in certain ways. You might see yourself as having changed so little that you are not much different from how you were ten years ago—and therefore, your aging is of little significance to you. Or have you so completely adapted to the idea of being a person aging in later life that you no longer react with surprise or denial to the fact that your actions are those of an older person? You may be clearly aware of it or only dimly so. You might view yourself as *somewhat* aged, but not *very*. You might protest your aging inwardly and suffer it silently, or shout about it loudly and complainingly. But at some time and in some way, you will have to come to terms with your aging in later life, as a chronological fact you cannot avoid. How you interpret this fact and what you do about it may influence how well you age.

What does it mean to *really* accept your aging? It means believing that "it has really happened to me. I'm part of the older generation. I'm an older man or woman aging in later life. I'm a senior, elder, older adult, or in the third age. No ifs, ands, or buts—I am it (old), and it is me." No matter what terminology (some of which is designed to keep you at a distance from your aging while some is there to "rub it in") you recognize, absorb, and live within the physical, chronological facts of your current existence. This means being clear about the things that have changed for you, especially physically. Nonacceptance means ignoring it, resisting or denying it, running away from recognizing it, and distorting or suppressing facts of your older physical being.

There are, of course, complementary attitudes that you might take and reactions that you might have besides acceptance or rejection. You might resign yourself in despair to the fact of your aging. Or you might give in to the inevitability of your aging with anguish and bitterness. Or you could try to develop full awareness and pay close and ongoing attention to the emergence and development of your aging processes. Thus, you might focus on becoming conscious of what is happening to you as you age. Or you might try to understand your aging in relation to your emotional and mental states. You may let the aging processes happen to you, or you may try to diminish, slow down, or resist them through exercise, medication, meditation, or diet. You might be frightened and resentful of the fact of your aging and that it is all happening too quickly. Or you might be quite pleased with it. You might deal with your aging realistically or unrealistically.

Whether you accept your aging as part of your natural life span, or instead resist it, will depend in part on your anticipation and your actual experiences of aging. If you expect it to be (or have experienced it as) miserable, difficult, and painful, you are apt to recoil from it and try to defend yourself against it by denying or ignoring it. If you expect older age to be a bummer, then you might attitudinally hold it off by self-deception, distortion, or delusion. On the other hand, if your aging has been primarily a positive experience, you might look forward with optimism to your aging in the future.

An acquaintance of mine accepts her aging enthusiastically by stating as she approached seventy, "Now I know what I was meant to be: an old lady!"

The question to be resolved is, how well does acceptance serve you?

ENDURING AND PERSEVERING

Aging in later life is a continuum of physical decline and dysfunction, whether rapid or slow. In either case, we must be prepared to deal with these physical challenges. To endure and persevere is to handle the difficulties of later life without letting them overwhelm you or override your desire to live in a particular way. This means that you *hold on* with tenacity and determination (to your positive attitude toward life); that you *hang in there* without giving up (fighting the adversity that plagues you, and not surrendering to passivity and hopelessness); that you *tough it out* (putting up with the pain, limitations, and frustrations as best you can); that you not yield to the pressure to withdraw; that you *ride it out* (absorb the adversity, expecting that the worst of it will be over soon); that you sustain the stress and distress (without turning into a cranky, bitter, difficult person); that you bounce back and manifest your resilience. To endure and persevere is to keep your psychic and emotional equilibrium despite the power and thrust of your difficulties—to be able to counteract the gravitational force of your burdens pulling you down. To endure and persevere is to continue your life under adverse circumstances with the hope and expectation that things will change for the better in the future, that you will grow stronger and better able to meet subsequent adversities as a consequence of having dealt with this one, that you will have learned much from your suffering—that is, if you hold on long enough and make continuing efforts to overcome, you will become a more potent, resilient person.

Refusing to give up and enduring the pains, pangs, and distresses of aging requires a lot of courage and determination. But going through it, persisting in your struggle, and insisting on enduring and persevering might very well bring you to a higher level of maturity. And enduring in grave crises might contribute to your spiritual growth and your humanity.

In his eighty-sixth year, my friend David was hit by a car. The impact on his body was so great that he was thrown into the air and landed some thirty feet from the point of impact. His legs were badly crushed, and he had a hole in his head. When he was taken to the hospital, he was semiconscious. When he told the physician that he was a teacher, the doctor on call, who happened to be an orthopedic specialist, changed his mind about how he was going to treat David. His original decision was to amputate both legs because they were so badly mangled. But he had a change of heart when he reacted to David in a person-to-person way. He then went on to operate for over nine hours, sewing up his legs and trying to restore them to a place where David might be able to use them again. Throughout this operation, David required several blood transfusions, but for a man eighty-six years old, he held up remarkably well, especially considering that he had to have his head sewn up. Six months elapsed from the time of the accident until he could go home. Over the first part of these six months, he was in a general hospital; in the latter part, a rehabilitation hospital. During his hospitalization, he had many friends, family, students, and colleagues visit him. But he also had much time to think, especially about his feelings on being a severely injured old man; to think about what in his life could motivate him to struggle against the pain and keep fighting to recover and live; to think about the future—whether he wanted one, what kind he wanted, and whether, in view of the uncertainty over his ever being able to walk again, he should continue to fight. What follows is a description, as told to me, of his struggle to come to terms with his accident and his life.

During the first week, David was in a state of shock, not fully able to focus on what had happened to him. When he could think a little more clearly and understand his plight and situation, he sank into a depression. Many of his friends rallied around him, tried to cheer him up, showed how much they cared about him, comforted him, encouraged him, and accepted his depression as a natural and inevitable consequence of such a severe accident.

As David slowly came out of his depression, he told me he felt profound regret that his life had been put on hold, that he had suffered a disaster and that he now had to put his life together in some way. He deeply regretted having to give up the travel plans he'd made with his recently met woman friend. But mostly, he said, he was ". . . afraid I'll lose her. Now that I am in such bad shape, why would she want to continue a relationship with me?" Despite his fears, his friend Jane was a faithful and steady visitor during his stay in the hospital and afterward.

David speaks to me of this psychic pain he suffers while immobilized in bed, waiting for his legs to mend. "I have a lot of impulses, a lot of desires, a lot of things I'd like to do, but I don't have the energy, and I don't know if I'll get it back." A short while after making that statement, he said this: "I'm old by the calendar, but not in spirit. I have a hard time keeping up with things. I'm not as clear as I used to be. Even my handwriting isn't any good."

In the rehabilitation hospital, David's moods swing from depression to fighting the depression, to feeling cheered up by friends, to a determination to get back to where he was, to uncertainty whether he could be the same as he was, to leaving it open on how he would be at the end of his recovery.

At the beginning of his stay at the rehabilitation hospital, he was quite impatient with the amount of time he had to spend in bed. When he got out of bed and into a wheelchair, he was impatient with the amount of time he had to spend in the wheelchair. Then, when he finally went home and used the wheelchair in his house, he was eager to walk with a cane. After walking with a cane for a while, he began to push himself to walk without a cane—at least a little bit, while holding on to the furniture. Although he was making progress, the progress was too slow for him, and so he kept pushing himself to do more and more, as much as he possibly could, despite the pain he felt in his injured legs.

Some seven months after his hospitalization and a short while after he had arrived home, he told me, "The whole situation still has a depressing effect on me. I fight against the depression by keeping myself busy. I ask people to visit. I initiate relations with people by the telephone. I get surprise visits that cheer me up. These visitors drive my concerns about myself out of my head. I am not blue or lonesome with good friends, because I have the pleasure and warmth of their company and I have a chance to express my love for them. Relationships are the prime movers of my life, especially my relationship with Jane. But when people leave, my concerns come back."

Along with using his friendships, he combats his despair by making plans for the future and keeping himself busy, cooking and reading. He also finds it helpful to curse himself while he's depressed, saying, "You son of a bitch! You lazy bastard! You hypocrite! You faker." He says that in this way he gets rid of his negative feelings, especially his anger about the accident.

Nighttime is an especially anxious time for David. He told me, "I lie in bed at night and throw unpleasant possibilities at myself and say to myself, 'What are you going to do when it snows? How will you walk with a cane then? I wonder if I will be housebound.' Then I say to myself, 'It isn't here yet, anyway, so why work yourself up into a tizzy? And I can't do anything about it anyway.'"

Reflecting on his accident, David says, "It broke the continuity of my life. It interrupted my teaching and my travel and all the things I used to do. The door to teaching is now closed halfway." (He has been asked to teach only part-time now. This is a great disappointment to him.)

Even though it is not clear how much use of his legs David will have, he works hard on his rehabilitation. "The accident changed me in a fundamental and profound way. It half killed me. I don't feel mobile or flexible. I feel diminished. I don't see how I can walk without a cane and without fearing I might fall."

At the time I interviewed David, some seven months after his accident, he was in a wheelchair most of the time. He practices walking a little while each day, and he rides his stationary bicycle. He exercises three times a week with a physical therapist and pushes himself to do more and more—so much so that at one time, when he tried to walk on his own, he fell and bruised himself. He refused physical help as much as he could and fought his dependency, even in situations where it might be advisable to rely on another person's arm. He has a strong feeling of independence, which he insists on preserving, always doing a little more by himself than is advisable.

David shows a lot of courage in fighting his depression and the urge to give up. His life energy repeatedly asserts itself as he galvanizes himself to improve his situation and continue to live and love. In evaluating David's activities, I cannot overemphasize the importance of his woman friend, whom he loves dearly, as well as all the friends who care about him. These friends call, visit, keep track of what's happening, encourage him, cheer him up, distract him, and gossip with him. They bring him information; they tell him what is happening to them. His male tenant, who lives in the upstairs apartment, lavishes attention on him, takes him places in his car, helps him in and out of his wheelchair, watches over him, and is someone David can always rely on.

David doesn't let the pain and the bruises and the nonuse of his legs hold him back. "I have to push myself because it's important. I endure the pain so I can walk. I won't give in to it. When I ask the question 'When is this going to be over?' it seems such a long way off. I want to go to Europe in August with Jane. I've got to have goals that push me. These are the motivating forces. I won't stop myself because it hurts. I face reality head-on and put up with it. I accept it, but this last accident was a little too much. Yet, I could have had both legs chopped off or been killed." He then seems to come to terms with the accident by saying, "It happened to me and I accept it as a fait accompli. I resent it. I deplore it. But I don't hate her (the driver of the car that hit him) for it. I know that once I start walking, all this will pass away. Nothing is forever." He seems to be accepting his fate. "I never had a sense that I was singled out for this tragedy."

In another mood, David said, "The accident was a downhill turning point for me. I'm not the same. I don't have the equipment or energy to start in again. I'm not fighting as hard as I should. Even though I am always pushing myself, I seldom feel I am doing enough. I'm hard on myself. Whatever I am doing, I feel that I should be doing more." He scolds himself and talks to himself in the third person: "You ought to be ashamed of yourself!"

He concludes his retrospective observations on his accident by saying, "There were times after the accident when I was full of frustration, restriction, pain, slow recovery, and unable to carry out my desires. I thought, why not let the end come. But I did nothing about it. After a time, my determination to get well came back. I'll never give up. I'll never give in."

KEEPING UP WITH MYSELF

How do I keep in tune with exactly where I am in the aging process? The issue is to catch up *and keep up* with myself. Changes occur, and I become a little different physically, emotionally, psychically, and socially. Only in retrospect do I recognize that I've moved from one place to another. And there is a gap between the time I become a little different and the time I recognize it. I wonder if I can close that gap. If I can achieve this, I might be able to act more in accordance with my capacities, realities, and limits at any particular time.

In addition to focusing on what is happening to you physically, you might try to become more aware of the changes in other domains. Are you less motivated to get involved with others because of diminished energy? Do you have a different attitude toward yourself? How do you experience your body changes? Have your interests or relationships changed? Is there a change in spirit or spirituality? Do you see life and other people differently? Has the nature of your thinking and feeling changed? Do you notice a decrease in emotional intensity, or has it increased? Are you still shocked and outraged at things that happen in the world? Do you believe that you are more vulnerable to illness and less secure physically? Do you find that as you get more insecure physically, you tend to focus more on your finances? As your eyesight fades and your short-term memory worsens, do you find yourself less interested in intellectual matters and events of the day, or do you struggle to keep up and keep sharp? Are you more patient or impatient than you were before?

Being aware of your aging process may mean that every day there is a new discovery, a new fright, a new adventure, or a new concern. Thus, you may discover a new disequilibrium, or a new bald spot, or a new sagging of skin, or a newly protruding vein. Or you look at yourself in the mirror and see yourself as older than you imagined. This observation can be a source of curiosity or insecurity. It can inspire an acceptance and embracing of the new you that is emerging, or you can emotionally reject it. However you react, you are noticing and keeping up with yourself and continuing to know who you are as you change over time.

With greater awareness of what is happening to you

as you age and change internally, you might be able to exert a little more control over your life and develop a clearer sense of how you would like to lead your life under existing circumstances.

DECLINE OF PHYSICAL POWERS

The issue here is how you handle the decline in your physical power and the slowing down in your physical functioning.

As your physical powers decline, your energy and stamina decrease, you tire more easily, you don't hear or see as well. You might overcompensate for these (1) by trying to be very busy, very active, very scheduled up and taking on more projects than you can handle; (2) by moving in the opposite direction and doing *less* than you are capable of; (3) by not getting involved, because you are "too tired;" or (4) by resisting projects and relationships because they "take too much out of me." Or, you might find a judicious balance between doing too much and doing too little, that is, doing just enough to fit your capacities and capabilities.

In addition to the experience of your physical decline, you will also react emotionally. You might become fearful about a new physical difficulty, and you also might begin to worry about its continuation and your further deterioration. You might become preoccupied with one or more dysfunctions and make them a source of worry and concern. You might agitate yourself by anticipating a miserable future that involves too much pain and suffering. Or you might accept your various declines in a matter-of-fact way, expecting them to occur and being able to adjust to them without too much difficulty. You might defend yourself against them by trying not to notice them. They might have a depressing effect on you, or you might become so ashamed of your dysfunctions that you want to withdraw from others. Perhaps you can become contemplative and thoughtful about them and approach them as a detached observer trying to note these emergent modes of functioning and their effect on you. You might reassure yourself by believing (as I do) that there is no necessary connection between your physical decline and any mental or emotional decline and that you can indeed retain your mental acuteness and compassionate feelings despite your physical decline.

WHO AM I?

How much did you search for identity when you were younger, especially in adolescence? But identity issues persist throughout life, and later life may be a time when you wish to redefine or reconstruct your identity or deal with still-pressing identity problems. Do you have a sense of yourself? Are you confirmed by others as being the person you feel yourself to be? Are you aware of any change in your identity of either a negative or a positive nature?

You might be aware of yourself as a distinct and separate person—a felt "I," an experienced "me," someone with inner depth—yet recognize that you share common attributes with the rest of the human race. Your identity might include an awareness of your roles—for example, as a friend or grandparent. This includes a sense of how you relate to others. If you have a firm identity, you might experience a sense of continuity, personal sameness, and connectedness with your past and with the people in your life. You might know where you come from, how you came to be, who you are now, and something about where you are going. You might see yourself as a specific kind of agent and initiator in the world, who knows inwardly who you truly are and acts in the world with that knowledge.

Knowing who you are often involves comparing your past and present selves and believing that there has been no major discontinuity between the two.

My friend David, even though he has experienced considerable physical change, had this to say:

"The major categories of myself have not changed that much. My feelings and attitudes have not changed. My expectations are just a little bit less. I am weaker physically and less capable of writing and working. I've seen it gradually coming on since age eighty—a diminution of energy. It's harder to get up in the morning and slower to get things done. Up to five or six years ago I chopped wood and ran. My weakness in hearing has been a setback. The functioning of my body is an important part of me, and that's changed since eighty. I don't have quite the enthusiasm I used to have. But I had the energy at eighty-two to make a seven-country tour, planning and organizing it. I couldn't do that today."

These continuities and reinforcements of the identity you are familiar with and feel good about can represent the positive aspect of your current identity. But as you age, negative features may make inroads into your identity—for example, the sense that you are a declining person with less energy and more dysfunctions, one who has lost physical, social, and mental power and efficacy. You see yourself negatively, as not the same person you once were. Or you feel strange and alienated from the self you once were. And perhaps most distressing to you would be the reality that you are someone with fewer years to live than you have already lived.

Questions arise: What would be a valid, appropriate, and realistic identity for a person in later life? How can I combine its negative and positive aspects into a harmonious balance? How can I maintain an identity that enjoys and responds to challenges, takes advantage of opportunities, and is intent on developing my personhood into ways of being a positive human being, striving to become the best person I was meant to be.

THEN, NOW, AND IN THE FUTURE

The issue is determining how to balance and combine living in the past, present, and future.

All of us live in three time tenses. The older we get, the more time we've lived in the past and the less time there is to live in the future. Yet the present is the only time we have to live in. If your past was much better than your present, you might daydream and reminisce about it, remembering the accomplishments, good feelings, and exciting life you once had. You might focus on the memories of the past, comparing them most favorably to your present circumstances. You might long for the past, see it as the most important and satisfying time of your life, and thus reinforce your dissatisfaction with the present. Reflecting on who you are and what you did in the past may be especially attractive and persuasive when the present is not so gratifying or appealing. Living in the past is a way of reviewing your personal history, of reclaiming a lost desired identity and trying to resurrect it in the present. It is also a way of reassuring yourself that you are significant in some way, to others and yourself.

On the other hand, you might focus on the present, on what is going on for you here and now. If the past was grim, you may need to forget it or construct a different image of it, expect not to repeat it, or derive some lesson from it. If you are someone who is very "present-oriented," you might feel that all you have is *now* and that you want to make the most of it and derive the most gratification that you can from it. You might appreciate and cherish your past, or you might see it as not completely fulfilling. You might either use the past or disregard it for your present purposes. You might not only relish the present but anticipate the upcoming moment with delight because you expect new happenings, surprising events, and continual stimulation to come your way, and multiple opportunities for being a mensch.

But what kind of eye do you have for the future? You can use your thoughts about the future to enhance the present, or use the present to prepare and plan for the future. You might be unconcerned about the future because you've done what you can and need to do about it. You may feel that the future will take care of itself. Or you may be concerned about the *brevity* of the future. You may have a number of expectations about who you will be and what you will do. These may be based on experiences you've already had, on foresight that is based on self-understanding, on unconscious fantasies, on predictions of your future based on your past, on beliefs about yourself and habits that you've long held or recently acquired, or on plans for a next career.

Our expectations are ways of anticipating and participating in the future so that we will not be completely surprised by it, will control it to some degree, and can reassure ourselves that we will be alive in it. Our expectations are also guides, influences, and determiners of our actions. Just as we often respond to others' expectations of us by doing and being what they expect from us, we also act in accordance with our own expectations, whether they are clear or disguised. Thus, they form the person we might become, by signaling to us what we should do and be, and what goals to pursue.

Since we can do nothing about the past and since the future is unpredictable, and because all we have at any moment is the present, it is of great importance to learn how to be in the present. This means that we are mindful of what we are doing and what is happening to us right now, that we absorb and assimilate these experiences and act on them. This means that we pay attention, trying to eliminate distraction and preoccupation, that we try to listen to the other for the meaning they intend, that we listen to ourselves, that we try to understand a situation as a whole. We remain alert and open to the nuances and subtleties of what is happening, and we respond with our understanding presence.

GIVING UP AND TAKING UP

As you age, the quantity and quality of your energy diminishes. As a consequence, you could reduce the wants and needs that you pursue. Or with increasing age, you might increase the number and kinds of wants or needs to make up for the deprivation and vulnerabilities that come with aging. Or you might do both at different times. Which pattern is yours? Are you clear about how much you've given up or lost and what you've taken up as a result? And with this clarification, have you determined what your limits are—what and how much you cannot do, and what and how much you *can* do?

How do you handle the things that have disappeared? (For example, a departed friend, a tennis game, an ambition, frequent sexual activity, diminished affection from others.) Are you replacing them or taking up new things as a consequence (such as more exercise, more thoughtfulness about your life, introducing meditation into your life)? Do you find yourself shedding interests, activities, and involvements more than you had anticipated, or increasing them more than you can handle? Do you miss the absent activities and people, and does their loss distress you? Does it arouse a sense of inadequacy or a feeling of diminished self-esteem? Or do activities from the past exhilarate you, give you a feeling of renewal, and reinforce your sense of competence, thus compensating in some way and to some degree for the losses?

THE PERSISTENCE OF TIME

Time is the vehicle that allows life to be lived. Time can have different meanings, a different "feel," a different sense of slow or rapid passage, at different times of your life and under different circumstances.

The issues are (1) your attitude toward, and feelings about, time; and (2) in view of these, how you spend and manage your time.

Here are some statements that reflect feelings and attitudes toward time in later life:

- Time is running out. Every day is part of the quick stream of time that flows so rapidly, I can scarcely tell one day from the next.

- I don't have enough time to do all the things I want to do.

- Time is short, and I mustn't fritter it away or waste a minute of it.

- Time moves so slowly that it hangs heavy on my hands.

- Every day is precious and to be cherished.

- Time is an enemy to be feared because it steals our life and brings us closer to the end.

- Time is a friend that shapes our life and offers us ample space to be who we are and do what we need to do.

- Time has moved so rapidly over the years, I can scarcely believe that I've lived them all. They've gone so fast!

- Time escapes me. I've got to learn how to manage it better.

- I have too much time on my hands, and I don't know what to do with it. I have to learn how to "kill" time.

- I'm so preoccupied with the little time I have left that I have difficulty in using it well.

- Time is a precious commodity that is available to me in only limited supply.

These statements reflect three different attitudes toward time: (1) Time is short, especially because the time left to you is limited and is so much less than the time you have already lived. (2) Time is viewed matter-of-factly, with no particular concern that it is passing too fast or too slow. And (3) time is chronologically short but psychologically and experientially long.

If you feel that time is short, that it moves too fast in view of all the things you would like to get done, and that you must use it as fully as you can, you might take a close look at how you spend your time. Think about how you might organize it to maximize your use of it, and then make some choices about how to spend it. Here is how you could proceed:

You evaluate and calculate what is worth doing and what isn't, according to your values, needs, beliefs, and obligations. What do you really want to do, and what can you do without even though you might enjoy doing it?

You set priorities among those activities that made the cut and are worth doing.

You determine how to budget your time: how much time to spend on a particular activity before you proceed to the next one. You can do this by careful scheduling, or you can come up with a set of general guidelines that have flexibility and variability built in.

Because you feel time is so short, you may become agitated or hurried. You then might have to watch out that you don't start flailing about frantically, act in a disorganized or confused way, or, at the other extreme, become frozen and immobilized. But dealing with time in a deliberate and organized way may help you feel comfortable with the passage of time, diminish the agitation, and help you enjoy the ways that you use time.

If time is of no great concern to you and you are not preoccupied about the speed of its passage or the brevity of its duration, you may undertake your tasks and spend your time leisurely, whimsically, playfully, or seriously. The choice varies with your mood, your circumstances, and the demands being made on you.

Finally, if you see the amount of time available to you as indefinite and each day as a renewal of that available time, then you might make time to appreciate the little things, or the big things, that come into your view. You might take time to concentrate slowly and carefully on the things you see, especially an object of beauty or something that especially appeals to you. You might search out its unique qualities and observe it intently. You might try to bridge the distance between you and it so there is no separation and it becomes part of you. And for a while, you might feel exhilarated by the power of the experience. Or experience the serenity and ease that comes with the sound of birdsong, or the wind in the trees, or the stillness of a dark night. You could feel the warm sunshine on your skin, or experience the joy of spring exploding in the trees and flowers. If you listen long enough, you might find the birdsong dissolving into you so that you and the sound are one. The passage of time becomes unimportant. Time appears to stop and keep you fixed in an eternal *now*.

Aging in later life also offers us considerable opportunities. This is the time when you can try to pull together various phases, experiences, and strands of your life—your ideas, imaginings, desires, and sense of self—into a coherent whole. By constructing a picture of your life span that encompasses the important events of your past and present, you might be able to find connectedness, meaning, and unity in your life.

It is important to come to some satisfactory resolutions with these issues of aging. If they preoccupy you or leave you conflicted, uncertain, or hesitant, they may very well interfere with your motivation and mobilization of energy to pursue the goals you've set for yourself, with diligence and effectiveness.

David gives me his attitude toward aging:

> *"I don't know what being old is. I think of myself as Davey, my mother's favorite child. I'm not aware of my physical defects and I don't think about aging. I think of myself as the same guy that I was. I don't regard myself as an old man. I have the same outlook that I had when I was younger. I make what concessions I must to my body. I don't run anymore and I don't swim anymore. I regret it, but it doesn't affect me. I see myself as the person I was: reasonably happy, fairly intelligent, capable, purposeful—a person with an interesting background and a life full of accomplishments."*

SEVEN

Coming to Terms

As we go through life, we all accumulate unresolved issues and lingering regrets. The older we get,
the more of these dangling issues we have. What we
wish to do about them, if anything, depends on how
they press on us; the emotional importance they still
have; our desire, need, or willingness to engage them;
and our anxiety and anticipated discomfort about
doing so.

Our progress in aging well and becoming the best
person we can will depend on the kinds of unresolved
issues we have and on how well we can come to terms
with them. Thus, a discussion of the ways that this
might be done can help us free ourselves to put more
of our energy into pursuing our goals.

I'll use the term "issues" for the problems, challenges,
contradictions, and regrets that remain unresolved and
still bug us—those that we feel need resolution and that
we wish to come to terms with.

By "come to terms," I mean reconciling ourselves to both old and recent issues that pain can preoccupy us and still carry a negative charge. Coming to terms with them includes finding a way to cope with them that is acceptable. For example, we sometimes would like to achieve a resolution with another person, or to mend a broken relationship. It also refers to dealing with problem situations we have been conflicted about and making peace with ourselves on these issues. Finally, it means handling a distressing issue in a positive way, that is, with a sense of achievement and a feeling of harmonious resolution. To come to terms with what remains unresolved, it's important to identify what issues are still relevant and emotionally charged—problems that have happened to you or that you have made happen. Coming to terms means resolving an issue to a sufficient degree that it doesn't continue to agitate us, interfering with the rest of our lives.

As I discuss some of these modes of coming to terms with various issues, some will be familiar to you. Others will not. From your point of view, different issues may require various modes of resolution. Or the same issue may be settled in several ways. Thus, different people will find some modes more effective or appropriate than others. The challenge is to find the best fit between the issue and the mode that will be most helpful in resolving and putting it to rest. What has prevented you from using your powers and capacities to the fullest? Resolving such issues may make it easier for you to realize whatever transformations you are capable of making.

What might you accomplish by trying to come to terms with the issues still agitating your mind and heart? You may be able to reduce the pain that accompanies an issue. Maybe you can heal the wounds you've suffered. You may find ways to be nurtured or to nurture yourself for the deprivations you've endured. You may better understand what has happened to you, what you've done, and what has been done to you. You then can be better prepared to deal with or prevent a next time, or not be so outraged or overwhelmed if it happens again. Out of the challenge and struggle to come to terms with an issue, you might develop greater peace of mind and equanimity, become more compassionate toward yourself and others, and develop greater understanding about the nature of the human condition.

Ways of coming to terms suggested here are not mutually exclusive, and they need to be undertaken over time. It may not be easy to come to terms with some issues. If you don't succeed at once, give it another try. After many trials, you might find some ways that work for you, and others that don't.

MOURN YOUR LOSSES

The issue: death of a parent.

Below is an illustration from my own life: grieving for my mother. It is a brief description of a long process.

When I was eight years old, my mother died. At the time, I was bewildered, disoriented, and overcome with grief. Sixty-six years later, I still remember vividly the recurring flood of tears that exploded from me at my mother's casket before the funeral began. I stood in the street numb and frozen. Each time a classmate or acquaintance passed by, I burst into a fresh set of tears. I couldn't fully understand or assimilate what was happening. All I knew was that I felt terrible, confused, and ashamed. I later recognized that some of my shame was related to my classmates seeing me in this bereft state in which I was somehow "less" than they were.

At this same scene, I remember a hysterical aunt wailing at me, "What will you do, you poor boy, without a mother?" This triggered wave upon wave of new bitter tears until the well emptied and I stopped from exhaustion.

Much later in life, I decided that these tears flowed out of a mixture of bewilderment, fear, great sorrow, and shame, with feelings of abandonment, insecurity, loneliness, and pity for myself. Indeed, what was I to do—what *could* I do—without a mother?

For the next few years, I remember going to the synagogue on the anniversary of my mother's death to say kaddish (the Jewish prayer for the dead). Here, too, the pity and sympathy from the congregation brought tears. As I grew older, though, more of these tears were held back. But there were still enough of them to leave me acutely feeling my sadness.

There was a long period, during my adolescence and early adulthood, when I didn't cry much. I assume that I was unconsciously following the male injunction that "big boys don't cry." Only many years later, I decided that big boys *should* cry. It will undoubtedly do them some good.

The next vivid memory I have is crying at various times in my psychoanalytic sessions. I began psychoanalysis when I was thirty, and I remember, when discussing my mother's death, crying small tears (that is, not many in any one session and not for very long).

In my early forties, various forms of meditation had been introduced in the United States as a practice that might calm the inner self and enable one to experience a form of spirituality. I worked at learning the practice for a year or two, and was in my second year of practice when I awoke early one morning to meditate. Instead, I started to cry. At first, I resisted the tears and struggled to keep meditating, but it soon became apparent that the tears took precedence over the meditation. They were insisting that I let them out. When I gave myself over to the crying, the tears came in a flood that continued for quite a while. Then there was a pause before another flood of tears washed over me. This went on for over a half hour for many mornings, during which I released copious tears, stopped crying until they were replenished, and let them tumble out again. This went on for a few weeks, three or four mornings a week. After each bout of tears, I felt cleansed, relieved, purged. I faced the new day with a lightness and relaxation that settled deeply into my body. I came to positively value these tears and their effects. On later reflection, it became clear to me that I was crying about the loss of my mother, whose death I had never fully come to terms with.

Sometime later, I attended a workshop in which I volunteered to reenact in a psychodrama a crucial scene around my mother's death. The facilitator of the workshop set up the funeral scene in a stark, realistic fashion, asking group members to role-play my family members and having one member represent my mother lying in her casket. No sooner had the scene been arranged and I said a few words about my reaction to it than I burst into a wail of "Why did you leave me?" and uncontrollable tears. I broke down into sobs, moans, and wails in an emotional seizure that overwhelmed me. I couldn't continue with the scene. I was held by a group member for many hours. During this time, I erupted loudly into intermittent torrents of tears. My body shook, racked with sobs, and the tears followed. The uncontrolled crying erupted again and again, with a few pauses in between. As I remember it, I don't think I stopped crying even briefly during those hours. My crying oscillated between subdued tears and peaks of weeping and moaning during that long period of being held.

Out of these episodes of weeping, it was brought home vividly to me that tears, if freely permitted and welcomed, could make an important contribution to one's coming to terms with a profound loss. I also learned that crying may have to go on intermittently over a long time before you can process some losses in a satisfactory way. It may be that we never fully come to terms with a profound loss, that we are never fully reconciled to it. The pain of the loss may lessen in its intensity, and the loss may diminish in its centrality, but the pain of it may never be completely gone. It also may be that the loss will evoke tears from time to time throughout our lives. Finally, I discovered that when I mourned for my dead mother, I was also mourning for myself and for the time when I would be able to stop weeping at last.

If one of your issues concerns coming to terms with the loss of an intimate, I recommend that you grieve or mourn whenever, and in whatever way, you feel the need to do so. Give yourself over to the grief partially, fully, or intermittently in whatever way seems right for you.

The history below illustrates some other ways of coming to terms with a different kind of loss:

For Joan Alton, a widowed high school teacher, the deepest pain is the loss of her only son, John, to a spiritual cult when he was eighteen years old. A child of the 1960s, he was seduced into leaving his middle-class home, disavowing his relationship with his mother, and living in the cult's group home. After some frantic attempts by Joan to get him to return, he told her in no uncertain terms that he wanted no further contact with her. Joan was devastated and had a very difficult time adjusting to this abrupt and harsh rejection. Any attempt she made to contact him was rebuffed. For the next few years, she gave up hope that she might ever get to see him again. At this point, Joan came to terms with this loss by becoming more nurturing and motherly to her students. She would spend much time with them, counsel them, have them to her house, virtually adopt some of them, and follow the careers of some after they graduated. During these years of noncommunication, Joan said to me, "I just considered him dead and gone, never to return." Despite her expectation of his continued absence, she had a strong urge to see him and try to reconcile with him in some way. After a few more years had elapsed, she tried to reach him and managed to talk with him by phone. However, during the conversation, John told her that he never wanted to see her again. In tears and brokenhearted, Joan surrendered to despair. She put more energy into her students and kept thinking to herself, "My son is dead." But she did not believe this completely, because a few years later, she again tried to reach him. This time, he agreed to visit her at home and did so, accompanied by a companion. Joan felt that the visit was prompted by John's wish to get money from her and that the companion made sure that John would return promptly to the group home. Joan refused to give him any money, because she knew that it would be turned over to the cult. John departed angrily. Joan felt bitter and resentful that he had not come to see her because he had any real affection or concern about her, but to extract money from her.

After this visit, Joan gave up any attempt to communicate with John. She came to terms with her loss, grief, and anger by trying to banish him *from her awareness, although she did think sadly about him from time to time. There was a long silence between them for a number of years until John's father died. Joan then contacted John and asked him to come to the funeral. He came briefly, again accompanied by a companion. He had only a minimal conversation with Joan and left immediately after the service.*

After this visit, Joan tried to reach John again by phone. This time, he was more receptive because he had married and now had a child, and he wanted his mother to see the child. Joan was again suspicious that a visit would be primarily to extract money from her. She nevertheless agreed to go visit John and his child in another city, where they were living. She was thrilled to see her grandchild and establish a relationship with her son. Over the next few months, Joan sent her grandson gifts and received pictures of him, and the tone of their relationship changed. It was now much friendlier, and John was eager to maintain and increase the contact. It soon became apparent that this change of heart was precipitated not only by the arrival of the grandchild, but also by the fact that the cult was breaking up and abandoning its group residence. Joan now had to come to terms with the fact that

John was now seeking a closer relationship, and she was not sure of his motives for doing so. She asked herself, did she even want this relationship after all the grief she had suffered at his hands? Was he sincerely interested in reestablishing a mother-son relationship, or was he maintaining the relationship because he was in difficult financial straits? Was he using the grandchild as a way to get more money from her? She kept her doubts to herself and accepted the more frequent visits initiated by John. The reconciliation was a slow, painful, and uncertain process. It lasted over the period of one or two years, and this time Joan is slowly coming to terms with her son and accepting him and his family. She is feeling good about being a grandmother. She is trying to put aside the pain she felt for some twenty years.

John and his family now visit every few months, and Joan welcomes these visits, longing to have a family that includes a grandchild. But she is still ambivalent. Her heart urges her to believe that the reconciliation is genuine and permanent and that she and they are indeed a family. Yet her head reminds her to be skeptical and suspicious that the reconciliation might just be a calculated way of getting money from her— either in the present or as part of the inheritance.

She has come to terms with her ambivalence by half believing and acting as if her son has been restored to her. But considerable suspicion and hurt still lingers in the background. Only time will tell how the ambivalence will be resolved. Will she finally come to terms with the ambivalence, or will she continue to feel both sides equally strongly?

Here are some other suggestions for mourning a loss:

Reminisce and reflect on your interactions with the deceased, identifying what you miss because of their absence and letting yourself feel the full extent of your pain. Spend time at the graveside, letting your thoughts and feelings take you where they will while you are there. Say a prayer for the dead in whatever form feels right to you, and wear signs of mourning, such as black, if that feels a helpful way to mourn. You may want to commemorate or memorialize the death of the person on a regular basis. While mourning the loss, take advantage of all the emotional support from loving friends and family. Talking with a friend about your sadness can lighten the load. And engaging in rituals that hold meaning for you is a time-honored way to affirm your sadness over the other's absence. You may feel the need to recite poetry about loss, death, and the end of things, or chant or sing sad songs that keep you in the mood of mourning, at least for a while. Reading about death and dying can deepen your awareness. So can getting together with others in a group who are similarly bereft, and talking about your loss. Express your feelings— especially your sadness—in writing. Try to describe accurately what you feel. Let yourself experience your feelings as deeply as you can. Recall conversations, experiences, and events that you shared, and the feelings that prevailed at the time.

While mourning the death of a loved one, you might also identify the ways in which you are also mourning for yourself: for the youth that is gone, for the parts of your identity that are diminished or lost, for the passions that have cooled, for the energy that has diminished, for the things and people who are gone and will never return, for the life unlived. You might find that you are also mourning the betrayals that tested your faith, the meanness you've endured and the meanness you've inflicted, the injuries you have suffered and those you have perpetrated, the things you never got but so badly needed, the unfulfilled longings, and the love unexpressed and love unrequited. You might also discover that you are grieving about many things you regret: things that you did wrong or could have done better; something that seemed right when you did it but turned out wrong; and activities that are no longer possible. You may find that you're also grieving the misunderstandings that separated you from others; all the disappointments that left their wounds; the unfulfilled desires that never found a home; the songs you never sang and music and poetry you never heard; the possibilities and potential you never realized. You might find yourself lamenting them all until you finally make your peace and shed the weight that hung so heavily and disturbingly over your mind and emotions.

ACCEPT WHAT WAS AND WHAT IS

The issue: a chronic illness or a decline in your physical capacities.

What does it mean to accept your declining physical state or your chronic illness fully? It means acknowledging what the situation is—not denying, resisting, or rejecting your condition. If you have a chronic illness, it means admitting to yourself and others, both cognitively and emotionally, that this is the case. After admitting it, you take it in and keep it as part of you. When you accept your illness fully, you and that disease are no longer separate, but are part of each other. By accepting it, you surrender to the unavoidable *what is*.

A series of steps might be involved in accepting your chronic illness fully. At first, you put up with the illness. You endure it with impatience or resentment, irritation, and the urge to fight it. Then you begin to accommodate or reconcile yourself to what you see as an inescapable affliction and an "outside evil" that has descended on you. You accept it partially. Later, you tell yourself that this is your reality, and you resign yourself to the existence of the disease because you know you can't change it. Reluctantly, you surrender to its "here-ness." Finally, you receive it into yourself and incorporate it until you are no longer fighting it and trying to reject it. When you are no longer agitated by the illness and are at peace with it, the illness becomes a familiar everyday companion. You automatically adjust to it, work along with it, find ways of accommodating it. Once you let your chronic illness be, it no longer pains you, you no longer resent it, and you admit that things are as they are. And you might then become content with yourself.

Acceptance is not about putting up with an event or occurrence, tolerating it, being resigned to it, and reluctantly giving in to it. If the acceptance is genuine, you surrender to the occurrence without reluctance, anger, despair, or indifference. This is not to say that you see the situation as desirable or something that you wished for. But once it has occurred, you take it in as something that *has happened to you* and is now part of you. In general, acceptance is allowing in all parts of yourself, even those you don't like or approve of—taking them in as aspects of yourself and trying to find a place for them. Acceptance includes such attitudes and sentiments as "whatever you have is enough;" "wherever you are is the place to be;" "whatever you are doing, you should be doing;" "whoever you are is the person to be;" "whatever you think and feel is all right to think and feel;" "whatever has happened to you must be absorbed and accommodated."

Here is how David accepts the decline in his sexual functioning:

> *"I reminisce. I fantasize. I yearn. But there comes a time in your life when you accept the irreversible and the inevitable. And the earlier you do it, the less you agitate yourself. It doesn't wreck my life, but it is a profound regret."*

FORGIVENESS: THE GREAT YES

The issues: the rejections by others that have pained you; and the injuries you have caused others.

It may not be easy to forgive others who rejected or demeaned you and caused you much emotional pain.

Nor is it easy to forgive yourself for the injuries you have caused others, or to ask their forgiveness. But it's worth a try. You might try to become more empathic and compassionate toward those who rejected you, and more understanding of their motives. You could ask yourself if you've misunderstood their reasons for rejecting you. You could at least consider the idea that they didn't know any better, didn't mean it, or couldn't help what they did. Or you may find other reasons that would help you excuse or absolve them, and you might thus be able to lessen the resentment you feel. Perhaps, you will discover that over time your bitter resentment has disappeared or diminished, along with your need for revenge. Or you may decide that you don't need reasons, excuses, or explanations in order to forgive them. You feel as though so much time has elapsed that this is what you really wish to do and can do for your own sake, for your own need to come to terms with them. If time has diminished the sting of the rejection or the hurt, perhaps you can now see the other person's positive aspects, and because of this you are ready to forgive them. Or you may simply feel that the burden of resentment is too heavy and you are ready to let it go.

Similarly, you may be ready to forgive yourself for the injuries and pains you have caused others. You might have many reasons, rationales, and justifications for doing so. Or you might just be ready to forgive yourself for no obvious reason, or because you now feel that you weren't at fault or didn't intend harm or that you did the best you could under the circumstances. You might deeply regret and feel ashamed of your "bad" behavior and vow never to repeat it. You might show compassion toward yourself and stop punishing yourself for what you did, telling yourself, "I was unaware of what I was doing;" "I didn't know any better at the time;" "I had no control over it;" "I was so immature at the time;" and "I know I wouldn't do now what I did then, because I'm a different person now;" "I've grown beyond such behavior;" "I now know that if I had to do it over, I would do it differently." You might feel the guilt and shame associated with your injurious acts and promise yourself that you will atone for them in some way, perhaps by doing "good works."

Asking forgiveness from another person will be a hollow request unless it is accompanied by remorse for having wronged the other. Asking forgiveness assumes that you can admit to yourself and others that you have perpetrated an injury and that you wish to atone for it in some way. You may feel distressed for having hurt the other. You may feel you had no good justification for doing so, even though there may have been provocation. You may decide to ask forgiveness after reviewing the event and discovering how injurious, in fact, you were. Because of the review, you may develop a new way of thinking about the situation and be prepared to ask forgiveness and hope that it will be given.

By forgiving yourself and others and asking forgiveness, you might come to see that we are all flawed and imperfect, that we all have a human, dark side, that we all (with very few exceptions) need to be forgiven for our weaknesses and shortcomings.

Some ten years ago, a close friend of mine moved to another city. We had known each other for eight years before she moved. Even though she lived in a different city, we kept closely in touch and shared our lives through letters and visits. After some ten years of separation, my friend moved to the same town I was in. I was delighted, expecting that our relationship would become even closer. To my great disappointment, it did not, even though my friend said she would like that. I was much puzzled by this and tried to understand the reason for the lack of development in the relationship. In thinking about it, I discovered that my friend had changed radically in attitude, style, values, and orientation toward living. I didn't view this change favorably, and on one occasion I told her so. I also told her I still had warm and friendly feelings toward her but that I did not like her as much now as I had ten years ago. This brought her much pain and a burst of tears. I apologized for making her cry but did not say more than that. Knowing that I had hurt her feelings, a few months later I apologized and asked her to forgive me. I told her that I did not feel it was my right to question her values, ambitions, and lifestyle. I told her I did not see these as "bad," but merely as different. I hoped she would forgive me for my attack on her self-worth. After some reluctance, a few months later, I felt that she had indeed forgiven me even though she never actually said so.

FORGET ABOUT IT

The issues: the slights, hurts, put-downs, snubs, and insults you have suffered from others.

At times, it is easy to agitate yourself over the slights and attacks on your self-esteem by others. Sometimes, it's possible to forget these intended or unintended emotional injuries in order to reduce your distress.

You might accomplish this forgetting by . . .

> . . . being willing to forget, blocking it out, or just letting bygones be bygones.

> . . . recognizing that the negative feelings that caused you pain and suffering in the

past have faded and no longer have the same meaning or strength.

. . . pushing them out of your mind and redirecting your focus onto pleasant memories or fantasies when the painful events or issues come into your awareness.

. . . letting the memory of these incidents fade. Avoid rehearsing, remembering, and reenacting them, so that the sharply defined picture begins to dissolve at the edges and become a dim image.

. . . "letting sleeping dogs lie." Try to avoid provocations that remind you of distressing incidents and feelings of lowered self-esteem. Stop the moving pictures in your head by distracting yourself whenever you begin to remember them and become agitated. Let yourself become deeply occupied with a task that demands your full attention and consumes your interest and energy.

. . . forgetting deeply embedded insults. This may be a difficult and tricky exercise. Remembering has an autonomous quality, and deliberately trying to forget may actually bring the issue into sharper focus. But you might find a way to *induce* forgetting or help you ignore the issue. And it's worth remembering that time itself is a powerful mechanism for forgetting.

JUST LETTING GO

The issue: ageism—being excluded from a work opportunity or organization because of your advanced age, and the bitterness, resentment, and humiliation that accompany this exclusion.

Besides by trying to forget, how do you let go of a hurt that is keeping you distressed? How can you come to terms with the issue by detaching it from your "self," thus making it no longer a part of your emotional space?

Of course, there are some things you might not be able to let go of, while others might be easier to let go. The intuitive skill lies in being able to distinguish one from the other.

There are lots of ways of "letting it go." You can try to diminish the issue's significance in your life by viewing it as a minor incident in your life span, enabling you to shrug it off and make it a matter of little consequence. Or you can try to transcend it by focusing on higher things that are of greater importance than these mundane matters. You can rationalize the situation by telling yourself that the position wasn't worth it if that's how they treat you, and therefore, you no longer care about it, and anyway it really doesn't hurt that much to have been excluded. Or you might recognize and confront the envy that you feel toward those who are already in the organization, and try telling yourself that these feelings are not worthy of you, or develop the expectation that this envy will eventually fade and disappear.

Rather than swallow your anger, you might be able to let go of it by really sinking into it and encouraging yourself to feel it deeply and fully. This could bring on a catharsis that will enable these feelings to "pass through you" and out of you. You will thus have cleansed yourself of that anger.

You might indirectly be able to settle the issue by getting acceptance, support, and inclusion from another group or individuals. Or you might see your attempt to get into that position as a way of not recognizing—though you do now—that you really wanted something else all along. And it is that "something else" you can now pursue. And also, you can now be thankful for being excluded, because it precipitated an occasion to learn something about yourself.

By deliberately and self-consciously making a determined effort to put the hurt aside—to shrug it off, push it away, or get rid of it—you don't deny its existence, but you try to remove it from a central place in your thinking and feeling. I don't mean that you selectively ignore or defensively deny it. Rather, you recognize that the issue exists, but you don't let it preoccupy you or interfere with your attempts to make progress in your career.

TALK TO YOURSELF (REALLY, IT'S OKAY)

The issue: a broken or antagonistic relationship.

It is possible to carry on a conversation with yourself and come away with a different view of a broken or antagonistic relationship. Review your memory of the events and sequences that led up to the break in the relationship. You might relive them by rehearsing the situation in your mind—the events, your feelings about the situation, what you said and did, what the other person said and did, how and in what ways you were involved emotionally, what such involvement might have to do with your past, how repeated and patterned your behavior was, and how analyzing similar experiences in the past might be helpful. Then you might try to visualize how you would like to have seen the situation proceed and how you would like to see it resolved now. Out of this dialogue with yourself, you may come to reinterpret what happened, and see it from a different perspective. You might see how you felt at the time, and what degree of responsibility you should take for the broken relationship. This might then lead to a change in your affect, to a resolution to try to mend the relationship, or to an internal coming to terms.

By trying to put yourself in the place of the other person and looking at the situation from their point of view, you might be able to develop deeper insight and greater detachment from the hurt that you feel. You might see and understand the situation from the other person's perspective and thereby reduce your own negative affect around the issue. Seeing it from the other person's perspective may enable you to make a significant change in yourself.

A member of a group I was conducting gave me this illustration. He recalled how antagonistic he had felt toward his stepmother when he was a child. He said he resented her because she favored her own children and neglected him, treating him in a hostile way. For this, he continued to hate her for many years. But some time in his adulthood, he reviewed the situation in his mind and discovered the reason for his stepmother's behavior. He now understood her behavior as similar to that of a bear protecting her cubs. He could accept and appreciate this and thus was able to let go of his resentment toward his stepmother. He felt he would have done the same in her place. In later life, he became friendly with his stepmother and proudly told me that she confided in him more than she did in her own children.

By ruminating and reflecting on the course of a broken relationship and the way it ended, you may come to change your focus away from the hurt feelings by asking yourself what you've learned about yourself, about others, and about your relationships. If you derive such knowledge from the situation, you might feel more positive about it and come to terms with it more easily.

TALK IT OUT WITH SOMEONE ELSE

The issues: the foolish mistakes you've made, and betrayal by a friend.

Talking with a sympathetic other who is willing to listen compassionately and nonjudgmentally might be a vehicle for enabling you to come to terms with your mistakes. It can also help you get past betrayal by another.

You might confess to them just how terrible, how remorseful, you feel about the foolish mistakes you've made. You might lament your regrets and describe how you have suffered because of your behavior. Through this confession, you might get sufficient relief from your inner pain to help you come to terms with the issue.

You might use your companion-listener to express your bitterness and resentment toward the person who has betrayed you. The important thing is to find the form of emotional expression that is most suitable for you in releasing the deep negative feelings that you have. As a consequence of this release, you may be able to put the betrayal, and the strong feelings it arouses in you, to rest.

MAKE AMENDS

The issue: coming to terms with a broken or disrupted relationship.

If you wish to make amends for a broken relationship that you helped break, you might, after you've recognized your remorse and regret about the situation, approach the other person and try to reconcile and make amends. You may have identified other feelings besides remorse and regret that motivate you to try to make amends, such as sorrow, shame, and a feeling of guilt. You may wish to apologize and express your chagrin to the other over your misdeeds. You might also wish to reveal how sorry you feel about the pain and injury you have caused the other. In addition to your genuine desire for reconciliation, you also must find ways of making amends that are acceptable and appropriate to the person involved. If, through contacting the other person, you discover that he or she feels much as you do and manifests a willingness and desire to bring about a reconciliation, you could then try to establish a framework of openness in which mutual apologies and remorse might be in order, and in which each person tries to speak freely about their shared (although not necessarily equal) responsibility for the break. You might want to persuade the other to identify with you the behaviors that made the situation difficult, and the feelings that were involved at the time. After this reciprocal expression and joint analysis of the nature of the misunderstandings and the different perspectives involved, you might explore what you can do to repair the relationship. Such an attempt to work out your differences might break through the anger and hurt and generate ways to begin coming together.

HANG ON, AND HANG IN

The issue: a difficult grandchild who is negativistic and rejecting.

The best you can do in coming to terms with a rejecting grandchild may be just to hang on, endure, and not give up on them. Don't let the situation dishearten you. You might demonstrate an abiding interest in the grandchild and offer help in an unobtrusive way. Your persistence and commitment to the relationship may eventually bring about a reversal. All that you might be able to do in the present is to make it clear that you are not reciprocating the rejection and that you are hanging in, into the indefinite future.

GROUP PROCESS

The issue: the loss of an intimate.

There may be a group in your neighborhood, or nearby, that is concerned with helping persons who have lost relatives or friends they were intimate with. This group may be of help to you in coming to terms with your loss. The shared viewpoints and pain, the expressed affect, the exchange of experiences and difficulties, the

reflections of the group members, and the group support might generate resolutions that did not present
themselves when you tried to come to terms with the
issue on your own.

REMINISCE AND RECOLLECT

The issue: a situation or incident that makes you
reflect on your life.

A review of your personal history provides an expanded
opportunity to recapture your memories of events, situations, and people. For example, you can relive in your
memory the vitality and energy of past times, making
them alive and real again as you reexperience them. You
can even change the pain of the past by retrospectively
putting a better face on it and seeing your life as more
acceptable, attractive, and joyous. You can free-associate
with your memories and use your fantasies to speculate
about what might have been, and enjoy the embellish-
ments and changes you now mentally devise. You can
try to do something creative with your memories by
representing them in a poem, a story, or some kind of
work that depicts them as being uniquely yours. You can
use and review your memories for the lessons they have
to teach you. You can trace your remembered thoughts,

actions, and feelings, the paths you have taken through life to get where you are. You can use your memories to compare with, and detach from, current experiences so that you can look at these more objectively. You can look upon your memories in anticipation of recounting your history to your grandchildren, who might be delighted to know about your past.

You can reminisce about the enjoyable, lovely things that happened in your life, and remember the times and places and people with whom you shared much joy. Remember, this was your experience, and it is part of you now.

When David was laid up with an injury from an accident, he reminisced about his past:

> *I live a great deal of the past—recalling and reliving all kinds of experiences. They came to me in flashbacks, maybe because I'm thinking of doing an autobiography. I have a rich memory, especially of my younger years. My childhood was idyllic; my mother was wonderful. I didn't get on so well with my father, but he was often away a year at a time. I remember especially my wife, my married years, and our travels together. I could summon up a trip we took: when we left, what ship we were on, where we went, and when we came back.*
>
> *Since I've had the accident, I spend a lot of*

time reminiscing about those early years because they were so pleasurable. It takes me away from the pain of my present existence. [Before the accident, he was very much present-oriented. But now, largely immobilized because of his injured legs, he does a great deal of reminiscing by telling me about his friendships, the wonderful times he had teaching, and the exciting events in his life. He then interrupts himself and says that he'd rather not be reminiscing but instead be engaged in his usual everyday life. I press him to tell me more of what he thinks about while he is in bed recovering.]

I think of my fifty-five years of a lively, happy marriage with my first wife [who died some three years ago]. I think about and realize that I am in love now [with a woman he knew previously but has only recently gotten close to]. I remember how proud I was to wear a uniform in World War II. To be a soldier was very satisfying. It meant I was a real man. I remember feeling so macho when we marched through a city in Italy. My thoughts were running this way: "If you mess with me, I'll let you have it." I was so astonished with this feeling of macho military force and this sense of power. I was ashamed of that feeling. I hated it. I never told anyone about it. It was so physical, so Nazi. It was out of character and I

*never had that feeling again. I look at myself as
a gentle person, as a maternal person. It was so
contrary to my gentleness.*

DO A LIFE REVIEW

If we expand these reminiscences, we can take a broader
view by looking into our entire life, accepting it as it was
and as it is, to try to find its meaning and coherence.
And who knows? We may come to a better understanding of who we are and what we've lived through. It is an
attempt to identify those issues and problems that are
still unresolved and that we want to come to terms with;
and to identify and use the wisdom we've acquired, the
humanity we've developed, and the spirituality we've
connected with, to improve the quality of our own
and other lives. With all this, we may develop a sense
of our wholeness of being and appreciate what unique
beings we are. With the understanding that can be de-
rived from this life review, we might develop some inner
peace and be able to put our issues aside.

The modes and mechanisms that have the least
chance of success in coming to terms with an issue are
denial, avoidance, pretending it didn't happen, and not
accepting responsibility for your behavior, instead putting the blame on the other person. You might even

try to deny that the situation had an emotional impact on you when, in fact, it did. Even if these mechanisms give you some sense of relief for the time being, the issue might come back to haunt you later on, after you thought it had gone away.

If some of your issues are so persistent and deeply ingrained that none of the modes described above work for you, you have a choice: (1) You may live with them undigested or unresolved the best you can. (2) You can seek specialized help from one of the many healers available to help you with their form of therapy. Or (3) you can try to discover your own ways of coming to terms with troublesome issues.

Now that I've emphasized the importance of coming to terms with your issues, I will give this caveat: You may find it useful, if one or another of your issues has unresolved residues, to leave them unresolved. For example, the residue of not having fully come to terms with a friend's death might be a poignant reminder of the fragility of life and the importance of living it fully now.

The way that you come to terms with your issues will affect who you are and how you live. This can be influential in how well you age. How you live and how well you age will depend on the kind of person you are. Thus, if you come to terms with your important issues and discover the best way to age in later life, this can contribute to your becoming the best person you can be.

EIGHT

Aging Well

While this whole book is about aging well, this chapter focuses directly on enhancing the quality and well-being we experience in later life. If you've gotten this far through the book, you know that aging is not a problem we need to solve, but a stage in life to be lived well. To blossom, we must be able to change into the indefinite future. Some of us would be content to put "aging well" as our only goal in later life. Others of us might see it as a necessary precondition for realizing more of our potential. Aging well and being a better person can be reciprocal: feeling good while aging, and feeling good *about* aging, can lead to being a good person and doing good. And being a better person can be a part of your aging well. Our task is to find, amid the difficulties and opportunities of aging, the best way to live our later life—one that suits our unique needs, interests, and capabilities.

However, there will necessarily be times when some

things are going well and others are not. My objective is to help you age better and weigh the balance toward the wellness side so that it comes to the fore in your life.

Aging well includes leading a good and fulfilling life and contributing to the welfare of others. Aging well is also a matter of how you see yourself in relation to your aging. In this chapter, I offer some suggestions that can help make your life more satisfying and meaningful.

First, we'll talk about some people who are currently aging well. Then, we will look systematically at what can make our later years good ones.

STANLEY AT SEVENTY-FIVE

Stanley is a dynamo of energy despite serious heart trouble that is now more or less under control. He is currently in such good physical shape that he can take the stairs three at a time. He has an all-consuming curiosity and interest in things, people, relationships, intellectual discourse, political events—just about anything that comes his way. He is a magnificent photographer and an exquisite gardener. He plays the cello, is a skilled carpenter, and knows how to deal with electrical problems. He mainly works as a psychoanalyst, and he devotes his time to treating patients, teaching and supervising students, consulting, and advising others in the field. In his spare time, he is writing a book that he believes will contribute to psychoanalytic theory. In addition, over a number of years he has created a series of medical clinics for poor and underserved people. He recruits personnel for these clinics, supervises them, raises money for them, and sees that they continue to function effectively. He is also deeply committed to his family and friends and keeps in close touch with his grandchildren.

Despite the recognition for his community work (he won an award for creating these clinics), he is a person without pretense. He ranks high in his professional field yet is humble about his accomplishments. He is most generous and giving and is ready to share himself, his ideas, and his knowledge, as well as financial aid for those in need.

Stanley continues to be an eager explorer. When he comes across a new situation, he engages it with intensity and curiosity, looking at it from many angles.

KATHLEEN AT EIGHTY-SIX

Kathleen is a widow and the matriarch of a family that includes her two children and two brothers, as well as many grandchildren, great-grandchildren, nieces and nephews, and grandnieces and grandnephews. She stays in touch frequently with members of the family by letter, phone, and personal visits and derives much satisfaction from her relationships with them. Several of her nieces visit her frequently and keep track of her welfare. For years, she has been the center of this family constellation, as well as a source of loans and gifts to members in need. She holds the family together by keeping communication flowing between them and thus helps them stay connected with each other.

Over the years, Kathleen has managed a business and several estates and has paid close attention to the stock market. She has become something of an expert on the stock market and spends a good part of the day analyzing stock movements, reviewing her portfolio, studying the various stock advisory newsletters, and making decisions about what securities to trade when.

Having lived her life in one city, she has many friends with whom she plays cards, attends plays and concerts and lectures, takes trips, and celebrates birthdays and anniversaries. These women have given each other support and companionship throughout the years. Yet Kathleen is intensely independent, lives alone, and tries not to rely on other people. Despite chronic illnesses, including a heart problem that requires a pacemaker, she remains a sturdy, interesting, and concerned person. Even though there are times when she has had much pain, she is uncomplaining and endures what comes her way in a self-contained, courageous, resilient way. She is a person who enjoys life, feels she has had a full one, and faces her future with equanimity.

MICHAEL AT NINETY

Michael is a spry, agile person who keeps an upright posture. He has an alert, inquiring mind and enjoys discussing political as well as intellectual events. Philosophy is one of his favorite subjects, and he likes to take on intellectual challenges. He reads a lot, especially in the field of history, yet that is not his major pursuit. His main interest is in painting, especially in watercolors, which he began in his seventies, after he retired. He lives alone, and painting and painting classes are the sustaining activities that keep him activated from day to day. He prefers not to rely on anyone. He likes to pursue his own path, doing his own shopping, cooking, and housekeeping on a fixed daily routine.

He takes considerable pride in being able to take care of himself, even though he does rely on his two daughters to some degree. His stamina and energy are remarkable for his age; for example, he doesn't nap in the afternoon. He feels that he fills his time in a satisfying way, although he doesn't have much interaction with others in his daily life. Not too long ago, he had a mild stroke, from which he recovered fairly quickly, showing considerable resiliency. He was soon back to his independent, self-sufficient ways, proud as ever of his independence.

GRETCHEN AT NINETY-SEVEN

Gretchen is a frail woman who has problems with her eyes, uses a walker, and has lived alone for the past fifty years. She exudes a sense of inner peace, despite her slow movements, physical limitations, and difficulties in getting about. She speaks slowly but with clarity of thought. She understands and responds appropriately to the remarks of others. She goes through her daily routine of rising, washing, and slowly dressing, taking a number of hours to accomplish these activities. She has breakfast with a neighbor who comes to visit her in the morning, but she spends most of the day on her own, listening to music and watching what is happening outside while sitting at her window. For exercise, she walks through the rooms of her house.

She is in touch with a few people, including her son, but does not have a great number of visitors—just a few neighbors who keep in touch with her. She cares for herself most of the time and depends on Meals on Wheels for hot food, and on a neighbor for shopping. Because of her poor vision and difficulty in walking, she doesn't get out unless a neighbor takes her for a ride.

Despite her limited contact with others, she doesn't

want anyone to live with her, nor does she feel lonely or go to bed wondering if she'll wake up in the morning. She strikes one as a comfortable, self-contained, relatively self-sufficient person with few complaints and an acceptance of her current existence.

CHARLES AND KELLY AT SEVENTY-SIX

Charles and Kelly have been married almost fifty years, and since their retirement they have led an active and contented life. Their primary personal involvement is with their two sons and their grandchildren, whom they visit frequently, even though they don't live in the same city.

They love to travel, using elder hostels as a way of seeing new places and meeting new people. They share many interests, old and new, but they each have their own interests. Charles loves to study languages and has mastered several over the years, while Kelly is an ardent birdwatcher.

They have many friends in their neighborhood, having lived in the same house for over forty years. For years, they have also maintained friendships with others living in distant towns. They are intellectually lively and keep abreast of what is going on in the political and social world, and continue to take an interest in the events of the day as well as in their friends' activities.

They are unusually open to meeting and engaging with other people, undertaking new activities, and looking for new and exciting adventures.

SUE AT EIGHTY-EIGHT

Sue is a small, verbal woman who has lived alone for fifty years. She has so many relationships and interests that she doesn't have time to do all the things she would like to do. She has four children and nine grandchildren, whom she telephones frequently; one close friend she is in constant contact with; and many friends and acquaintances she sees less often. Although she enjoys long conversations, she is not demanding of attention from others.

She is a member of a library group and a church, as well as other groups. She maintains an interest in public affairs, listening faithfully to National Public Radio every morning, and takes special interest in causes such as peace, energy conservation, and antinuclear activities. She supports deprived children financially and keeps in contact with them by letter.

Despite her extraordinary energy and enthusiasm, she requires twelve hours a day of bed rest and cannot walk much because of weakness in her legs. Nonetheless, she either drives herself or is driven to various meetings she attends weekly. She values her many relationships but doesn't want anyone to live with her or intrude on her privacy. She is self-reliant, having successfully managed her financial affairs for the fifty years since being widowed. She values her independence so much that when a physician recommended she stop driving, she was so outraged that she discharged him! She continues to drive.

She reports that she is not particularly introspective, but very curious and continuously learning. She is quite content with her life and rarely is depressed, "because I have nothing to be mad about." She expresses optimism and cheerfulness in her welcoming approach to other people and in her unusual variety of activities and interests. Her conversations are cogent and rational. Although she enjoys engaging others in long talks, she is nonetheless a reserved person. She has many friends who call on her, but she is not demanding of their attention. Rather, she is such an attractive person that they are impressed with her and want to be with her.

JOAN AT EIGHTY-NINE

Joan is an attractive and compelling person who lives in an apartment in a large village for senior citizens. One of her outstanding characteristics is her determination to control her own environment and as much of her life as possible. Many people in her housing complex admire her, value her friendship, and vie for her attention. She has many appealing qualities and a great deal of charisma. People flock around her at social gatherings, greet her warmly, and treat her like a celebrity. Although she can take care of herself, those she meets are eager to offer her some help, which she turns down. She relates to others in a sweet way, yet is a forceful presence. She is also a person of integrity who takes her responsibilities seriously and keeps her word whenever she gives it. In some situations, she can act quite queenly, showing herself to be a strong-willed, determined person who likes to have her way but is not objectionable in the process of getting it. She is also a center of interest to her own children, who keep in frequent touch with her.

Even though she is less than five feet tall and weighs somewhere between ninety and a hundred pounds, energy flows out of her. This may be in part because she has devoted her life to exercising. Currently, she exercises two hours a day and teaches exercise routines: how to breathe, how to walk, how to maintain the body, how to stretch and bend, how to exercise the eyes. In addition, she has taken on a class of Alzheimer's patients whose illness she believes she can affect through exercise. In this way, she shows perhaps unwarranted optimism, but also a deep faith in her capabilities. She projects energy in her walk, her talk, and her numerous activities.

Over time, she has had various spiritual teachers,

both Eastern and Western. At present, she is devoted to the rabbi who conducts the services in her village. She attends services faithfully, meditates, and visualizes positive things for herself. Her great cause is the value, both spiritual and physical, of various exercises, especially breathing exercises. She believes herself to be a healer and claims to have healed quite a few people.

She likes many people, avoids those she doesn't like, and fights with no one.

Although the people I have known vary widely in age, physical health, education, work, and involvement with others, it is possible to derive from these sketches a sense of what it takes to age well. From talking to such people, I have come to the conclusion that aging well includes several important elements. Not all these elements are necessary, but it seems that the more of them that are present, the better one ages.

To age well, we need a reasonable degree of mental and physical health, and cognitive capacity to think clearly. We must have a strong sense of independence and insist on preserving it. We need positive, warm, loving involvement with one or more friends or family members, and we need to feel reciprocal concern and caring for others. Projects that contribute to our own and others' well-being are a meaningful way to stay connected. So is work that we love and care deeply about. Eagerness, curiosity, and openness to learning are key. With our sense of wonder engaged, we may build on the knowledge and skills we already have, or expand our interests in new directions. By having both short-term and long-term goals, we can stay excited and motivated to get outside ourselves. Other hallmarks of aging well include enthusiasm, persistent high motivation, activities undertaken energetically, and an inner sense of calm and peace.

Here are some suggestions for aging well. Implicit in them are injunctions to act, tasks to undertake, attitudes to adopt, goals to pursue, qualities of character to develop, and subjective states to strive for. Any of these, in any combination, can contribute to our aging well.

GROW, ADAPT, AND DEVELOP

To be happy, we must think of ourselves
as in an unceasing process of becoming.
—Avis Carlson quoting Dr. Herbert
Kelmme, from *In the Fullness of Time*

View yourself as someone in process, and take the opportunity to grow wherever and whenever you can. See yourself as in the process of becoming a little different self sometimes. Permit yourself new flights of fancy. If you can see yourself as unfinished, it means you're evolving all the time.

Encourage your curiosity to awaken and guide you to new possibilities. As the world gets worse, you have to get better. Cope with it and make it better.

Many of us suffer from repressed tenderness. If you do, find ways to express it directly to someone you care about.

Complete those aspirations that you have not yet realized. Become aware of your unlived life and begin to live it. Find and reenergize the lost, unexpressed, and unrecognized parts of yourself that are longing to come out. Ask, *Who and what might I yet become? In what ways can I still be productive, creative, and useful?* Become more of what you intend and what you can be.

View yourself as a student, always in the process of learning. If you view each situation you are in as an opportunity for learning something, you'll never get bored. As a perennial student, you'll constantly renew and awaken yourself.

Broaden your horizons; enlarge the scope of your thinking and feeling; deepen, stretch, and expand your imagination; grow the vision of what you can do. Unfetter your empathy. Who else can you learn to understand

and care about? Don't let shyness, modesty, or short-sightedness prevent you from pursuing noble causes, from being magnanimous, from being adventurous and seeking peak experiences.

Renew, reinvent, and revitalize yourself. Acquire knowledge that empowers you and improves the quality of your life.

BEAUTY IS TRUTH

There is beauty all around us, just waiting to be appreciated, enjoyed, experienced, and intensely felt. Taking these moments in heightens our capacity to maintain an open, interested, and aesthetically rich life.

I jotted down my appreciation of a commonplace sight:

TREES
I LOOK OUT MY WINDOW AND SEE A
TREE. IT HAS A COMPANION BEHIND
IT NEARLY AS TALL. BOTH ARE HUGE,
TOWERING OVER THE HOUSE ACROSS THE
STREET. I LOOK AROUND AND SEE TWO
OTHER TREES, ONE TO THE RIGHT AND

ANOTHER ONE TO THE LEFT. IT'S NOT A FOREST BUT A SUBURBAN STREET WITH A FEW TREES HERE AND THERE. I FOCUS ON THE TREE DIRECTLY IN FRONT OF ME AND NOTICE ITS BRANCHES. SOME GO STRAIGHT UP, SOME LEAN SIDEWAYS, AND THERE ARE MANY OF THEM, SO MANY THAT I CAN'T MAKE OUT HOW MANY OTHER TREES THERE ARE. IT IS SPRING, AND THE BRANCHES ON THE TOP ARE HEAVY WITH LEAVES, FLOWERING IN GREAT PROFUSION. AT LEAST, IT SEEMS PROFUSE, BECAUSE THEY ARE BUNCHED AND CLOSE TOGETHER AT THE TOP. THE LARGE BRANCHES ALSO HAVE SMALLER ONES THAT BRANCH OUT FROM THE INITIAL BRANCH, AND THE LEAVES ARE GROWING ON THE SMALLER ONES. THERE IS A SLIGHT WIND THAT SHAKES THE LEAVES AND STARTS THEM SWINGING EVER SO LIGHTLY IN THE BREEZE.

I TAKE IN THE LARGER SCENE AGAIN, AND THE PROFUSION OF GREEN AFFECTS ME IN AN ENTRANCING WAY. I BEGIN TO THINK ABOUT THE NEW

LIFE SPRINGING FORTH. THE TREE TRUNK LOOKS SO ENFEEBLED AND DARK COMPARED TO THE VITALITY AND BRIGHTNESS OF THE LEAVES. HOW INTERESTING THAT THIS TREE SHOULD PRODUCE THESE LEAVES NOW! HOW INTERESTING AND WONDERFUL AND TRULY INEXPLICABLE. THE TREE LISTS A LITTLE BIT TO THE RIGHT, BUT IT IS FAR FROM DECREPIT AND WILL NOT FALL. I EXPECT IT WILL BE AROUND FOR QUITE A FEW YEARS, UNDOUBTEDLY LONGER THAN I.

I LOOK AT MYSELF LOOKING AT THE TREES, AND I TELL MYSELF THAT I'M NOT SURE WHETHER IT'S AN OAK OR SOME OTHER KIND OF TREE. I FEEL MYSELF DWARFED BY THE TREE EVEN THOUGH I'M NOT UP AGAINST IT. IT SEEMS SO HUGE. I BEGIN TO REGRET THAT I'VE SPENT ONLY SHORT PERIODS OF TIME LOOKING AT TREES AND NATURE. I MUST DO MORE OF THAT.

Archibald MacLeish had a similar reaction to natural phenomena:

With Age Wisdom

> At twenty, stooping round about,
> I thought the world a miserable place,
> Truth a trick, faith in doubt,
> Little beauty, less grace.
>
> Now at sixty what I see,
> Although the world is worse by far,
> Stops my heart in ecstasy.
> God, the wonders that there are!

Similarly, evoke whatever creative impulses you have in any area. Whether cooking, gardening, or painting a landscape, try to create something new, or a new combination of things. Whatever you do, keep alive the impulse to contribute something new to the world, and you will renew yourself in the process.

Here is how Connie Goldman puts it:

Creativity is a mysterious thing. It's an attribute of every human being, not just the great and the gifted, not just the young. Age can bring an enriched sense of self, and often, people are more creative in their later years. Creativity is the expression of the human spirit—to be studied, cultivated, and cherished.[21]

STAY OPEN, BE FLEXIBLE

Have an open heart. Include others in an empathic, compassionate, and caring way and accept their emotional states. Have an open mind: be receptive to new ideas and experiences, and pursue those experiences you would like to have but were reluctant to try.

Recognize that aging in later years is uncertain, perplexing, and unpredictable. (There will be an end, but when and how?) So be relaxed about discovering the best way to deal with uncertainty.

Let the child in you come out and play when you can and when you don't feel too foolish. Life is too short to be a grown-up all the time.

---

21 Connie Goldman, "Late Bloomers: Growing Older or Still Growing?," *Generations: Journal of the American Society on Aging*, no. 2 (Spring 1991), 41-44.

RESPECT YOURSELF, RESPECT OTHERS

And expect others to give you the same respect. Find people who value you for the unique person you are and who enhance your self-respect. Have a positive regard for yourself. Affirm to yourself the value and meaning of your existence and your lifestyle.

Treat yourself well. Be kind to yourself. Accept your foibles, forgive yourself for your mistakes, and don't punish yourself for not being better than you are. Do gently expect yourself to become better over time.

Feel your pride and power, whatever your age. Assert your personal power when it is necessary and appropriate, and help others do the same.

Don't knock yourself out trying to get back to where you were when you were younger. Appreciate yourself for who you are now and for doing what you can do now. Honor yourself without ignoring your flaws and limitations.

STAY INVOLVED IN, AND WITH, LIFE

Stay attached to what involves you, and stay fully present with all that happens to you.

Keep your interest in life ongoing, and at the most

intense level possible. Participate with enthusiasm and passion in whatever is going on with you. If you feel "out of things," seek out situations where you can get involved. Keep yourself alert and excited about new possibilities for being involved.

Barbara Meyerhoff, in her book *Number Our Days*, describes someone she studied:

> *He was a man searching, always searching in everything that went on, for what life is about. He was a model for us in getting old. It is not necessary for us to be lonely and feel sorry for ourselves . . . We can learn how to live and how to die from him, calmly but vigorously, members of life to the very last minute.*[22]

Listen to Bernard Berenson at ninety-two:

> *Living at my age with all my disabilities is anything but a picnic. So why cling to it? Partly out of mere animal instinct. Partly out of curiosity about tomorrow and day after*

---

22 Barbara Meyerhoff, *Number Our Days* (New York: Simon & Schuster, 1980), 75.

tomorrow. Partly because I am not resigned to giving up, and still am eager to achieve, if only as an inspirer . . .

But I still want to learn, I still want to understand, and I still want to write. How shall I get rid of these lusts? Physical incompetence only will emancipate me from their slavery, but what kind of freedom will it be? The antechamber of the End. But how I still enjoy sunlight, nature, and stormy skies, and sunsets, and trees and flowers, and animals including well-shaped humans, and reading, and conversing!

JOY OF LIFE

Permit yourself to be joyous, even ecstatic, whenever you can. Every day, find something to laugh about. Let the laughter "fill you up" whenever it occurs.

Be playful and have fun in circumstances that are appropriate. Look for the humor in a situation. Be nonserious and take things lightly often so that you don't feel yourself to be a dour person.

EXPLORERS HAVE MORE FUN

Old men ought to be explorers
Here and there does not matter
We must be still and still moving
Into another intensity
For a further union, a deeper communion
   —"East Coker" by T. S. Eliot
     in *Four Quartets*

Often standing in the way of exploring new horizons is a fear to go beyond the limits, to break the boundaries of the expected and conventional—the fear that we will become distressed, destructive, or mad. Yet that may be precisely where the creative, the ecstatic, the exhilarating is to be found. So don't be afraid to be in transition. Become more accepting of unfamiliar and changing situations.

Become an explorer: open up to being transported beyond yourself and being moved by a great passion, a noble act, or a burst of creativity. Delve into remote areas and foreign lands inside yourself, unfamiliar thoughts and ideas, strange imaginings, and new affective realms. Undertake new tasks and welcome the opportunity to engage in new challenges.

Seek out situations that provide security, but not only those. If you seek out situations that are risky and uncertain, know what you are doing and how to retreat to a safe base.

The quest for adventure knows no age. We are never too old to decipher tantalizing mysteries and puzzles.

HANDLE ADVERSITY

Shrug off the put-downs, aggressions, and power plays that others try to impose on you. Learn how to handle these annoyances so they don't raise your stress or anxiety levels. Let them wash over you, or actively push them away.

Be strong on the outside, doing what is needed and handling unpleasant or difficult situations, and warm and tender on the inside, being nurturing when needed.

Since illness and other adversities are unavoidable in later life, learn how to handle them. This means not making your illness your central focus. It also means putting it aside and going on with the rest of your life. Focus on your illness only during those times that you need to treat it so that it doesn't get out of hand. Try to resist the depressive power of the illness by taking a positive attitude toward your own recovery. Embody a "fighting spirit," filled with courage, dogged determination, and the conviction that you will conquer the illness—that you will endure, using all your means, from medication to meditation, to reverse the illness process. Don't give up hope.

Relentlessly pursue health with a willingness and the stubborn will to continue to fight a disease. Genuinely believe in and expect an improvement or recovery. Thus, in addition to doing what is medically necessary, you will exert all your powers of mind, heart, wish, belief, spirit, and behavior to defeat your sickness. You will also accumulate inner strength to deal with the vicissitudes of aging.

Convert your adversity into a learning experience and use your recovery from it to develop resilience. Use your years of handling adversity to develop effective coping skills. Bring your attitudes, mental strength, and knowledge together to optimize your ways of dealing with adversity.

John Neihardt, in his book *The Giving Earth*, tells a story about a Sioux elder who was recounting his experience as a youth on a vision quest. The old man said, "As I listened . . . a power ran through me that has never left me, old as I am. Often when it seemed the end had come, I have heard the eagle's cry—*Hold fast, hold fast; there is more . . .*"[23]

On November 8, 1993, the *New York Times* published a story about Mavis Lindgren, eighty-four, who is a

---

23 John G. Neihardt, *The Giving Earth* (Lincoln University of Nebraska Press, 1991), 273.

long-distance runner, participating in marathons all over the country. She began running at the age of seventy. In one of her marathons, she fell and broke her wrist but finished the race anyway, with another person running at her side, propping her wrist up.

BE COURAGEOUS

Find the courage within you, sustain it, expand it, and keep it ever handy to confront and grapple with the "slings and arrows of outrageous fortune." Be courageous not only in dealing with adversity, but also in facing and embracing later life in general.

In the poem "Courage," Anne Sexton wrote,

> when you face old age and its natural conclusion
> your courage will still be shown in the little ways,
> each spring will be a sword you'll sharpen,
> those you love will live in a fever of love,
> and you'll bargain with the calendar
> and at the last moment
> when death opens the back door
> you'll put on your carpet slippers
> and stride out.

Eleanor Roosevelt said of herself, "I think I am pretty much of a fatalist. You have to accept whatever comes, and the only important thing is that you meet it with courage and with the best that you have to give."[24]

MAKE YOUR LIFE MEANINGFUL

Newbery Award–winning children's author, educator, and thinker Elizabeth Gray Vining, who authored over sixty books in her life, emphasized that life is to be cherished. She saw it as a sacred trust: "It seems to me childish and churlish to say that life is horrible and without meaning. Life is a trust, given into our hands to hold carefully, to use well, to enjoy, to give back when the time comes."[25]

Embrace and reinforce the meaning that is already present in your life. If it isn't there, create some!

Maintain meaning in your life by making meaningful whatever you are doing at the moment. The process itself, whatever it is, can be as meaningful as the expected result.

Search for meaning in its larger sense. What is

---

24 David Michaelis, *Eleanor* (New York: Simon & Schuster, 2020), 526.
25 Elizabeth Gray Vining, *Being Seventy: The Measure of a Year* (New York: Viking Press, 1979), 168.

ultimately and existentially meaningful? And in its smaller sense—find the meaning invested in the details of everyday life.

STAY RELATED

Stay related to people of all ages, both older and younger than yourself. And make some connection with your community and the larger world. Especially, stay related with those who admire and respect you.

Get to know someone older than you whom you admire because they're aging well and who can serve as a role model for you. And pay something forward by serving as a role model and sharing your experience and wisdom with others who are receptive and welcoming.

Learn how to help your grandchildren fulfill their potential without alienating their parents—or, better yet, with enthusiastic approval from their parents.

Have warm, friendly relations with as many people as you can, and feel a sense of personal responsibility with them. But also protect your private space from intrusion when you need to.

Develop effective means for resolving interpersonal difficulties. Express your feelings of frustration, disappointment, and irritation without doing injury to yourself or anyone else.

Staying connected takes some effort, but it's worth it.

COMMIT TO A PROJECT OR CAUSE

> *If we are to make appreciable headway, persistence is indispensable. People who achieve greatness are almost invariably passionately invested in some one thing. They do a thousand things each day, but behind these stands the one thing they count supreme.*
>
> —*The World's Religions*
> by Huston Smith

How stimulating and life-enhancing it is to fight for a cause—a consuming interest that wakes you up in the morning and keeps you energized during the entire day. Find something you wish to pursue passionately, and devote yourself to it with care and concentration.

A Salvadoran had long worked with a labor union to improve the lot of poor people and push the country a little closer to being a democratic state. He was picked up by the Salvadoran military, who were ready to assassinate him. They put a gun to his head. But they didn't shoot the man—they were merely trying to frighten him. After his release, he reported that when it appeared that he would be executed, many thoughts ran through his head, especially anguish and despair about his wife and young children being deprived of a husband and father. But he said he had come to peace with himself and was able to accept his impending death calmly once he recognized that after his death, others would pick up the banner and continue to work for the causes he was sacrificing his life for. This overarching cause made his life worthwhile and enabled him to come to terms with his death in a courageous and accepting way. For him, this cause was larger than he was. It was something to believe in, to work for and, if necessary, die for. After his release by the police, he continued to work for his cause.

To be curious, challenged, and engaged in a project, using your energies constructively on something that is meaningful to you, is to fill your day with purpose. It may be similar to or different from the work you did in your career. Keep working at projects that stretch you, involve you, push you. Keep working at what you love to do. Participate fully, joyously, and energetically in these activities. The process of *doing* a project can be more exciting and more satisfying than achieving the result, and more important in igniting your enthusiasm and motivation.

Projects, big and small, can constitute your raison d'être from day to day. They can serve as a focus for your thoughts, fire your imagination, concentrate your energies, generate innovative ideas and insights, and help you discover new ways of seeing. If a project is important to you and you commit deeply to it, it can become an organizing point of reference for a good part of your life. To be engaged in projects large and small is a way of being engaged in *life*. Without them, we feel at a loss, drifting, even useless. With them, we become alive and energized.

Seek out and develop a stimulating environment for yourself with people and projects that keep you engaged. Work toward a higher cause or purpose that is not for your immediate benefit, that is bigger than you, and that contributes to the welfare of others. We know of many famous people who aged well: Freud, Picasso, Berenson, Michelangelo, Leonardo, Jung, O'Keeffe, Grandma Moses, Arthur Rubenstein, Vladimir Horowitz, John Dewey, Bertrand Russell, Albert Schweitzer, Martin Buber, and Einstein are but a few. They aged well primarily because they were passionately committed to their art, music, philosophy, and projects and conceived of themselves as pursuing a higher purpose.

In his late eighties, Bertrand Russell led a nuclear disarmament movement in the UK. At the age of ninety, he offered his services to heads of government during the Cuban missile crisis. Until he died at age ninety, Albert Schweitzer cared for patients in his hospital in Gabon. "Too old" was not a phrase in their vocabulary.

USE YOUR FREEDOM

In retirement, freedom is there for us to use as we see fit. The challenge is to identify the *ends*—what to use our freedom for—and the *means* for pursuing these ends, and then develop the plans and actually carry out these plans. The most important thing is to use your freedom to express your inner self—the self that has long been repressed, the self that has been afraid to come out.

PROTECT AND ENHANCE YOUR PHYSICAL AND MENTAL HEALTH

When a speedy life with too much to do and too little time causes stress, learn how to slow down. If your life is slow and dull, with too little to do, kick it into a higher gear.

Care for yourself, not in an obsessive way but in a thoughtful way. Make sure that your body gets the right food, rest, exercise, and clean air. Avoid emotionally noxious and destructive situations. If a particular setting or group of people makes you feel anxious or unworthy, consider being somewhere else, with different company.

Keep moving physically, mentally, and emotionally. Movement is evidence of vitality and life force. Rest should be a renewal, a temporary stopping place.

As you change physically, emotionally, mentally, and spiritually, keep up with yourself so that you know where you are, when you have had enough of something, what your limitations and constraints are, what you can pursue, and what you must decline. Release gracefully the things that are no longer accessible or possible for you, such as running a marathon, or staying awake all night and expecting to be fresh the next morning.

Find internal and external places where you feel relaxed, centered, and at peace with yourself and the world. Stay there as often and as long as you like.

STAY POSITIVE

Don't get preoccupied and overwhelmed by your issues and regrets. Live in the present as much as possible.

Don't give up on anybody, especially yourself. Where there is life, there is hope.

Be constructive, and accentuate the positive. This doesn't mean that you ignore or deny the negative, only that you assess the circumstances and be as positive as you can.

Learn how to handle the destructive elements that descend on you. Instead of letting an anguishing, distressing, or anxious situation burrow deep in your gut, see if you can raise it from your gut to your shoulders, and then shrug it off.

Say yes to life, and maintain a life-affirming attitude. Resist despair. Cultivate a love of life and continue to care about what is happening to you and others. Remember that life matters—no matter what. Maintain the attitude that you make a difference. Avoid or minimize negativity: cynicism, carping, criticism, complaints, and blame.

Maintain a reverence for all life and a respect for nature.

Fight your resistance to looking into the future. Make realistic plans for the future. Enter it enthusiastically and expectantly and see it as part of your present.

Review your life. Recall its peaks, joys, and transcendent moments. As you live through your life span, get a sense of your journey and a sense of wholeness as you approach its completion.

Be selective in how you use your time.

MAINTAIN A HIGH ETHICAL AND MORAL STANCE

*I speak truth, not so much as I would, but
as much as I dare; and I dare a little the
more as I grow older; for methinks, custom
allows to age more liberty of prating, and
more indiscretion of talking of a man's self.*
—From *The Essays of
Michel de Montaigne,
Book the Third*,
translated by Charles Cotton

Seek authenticity. Be true to yourself and truthful to others. Act with integrity. Try not to be a calculator or a manipulator, to cut corners, chisel, or bend the truth for personal gain. Be real, open, and expressive of your inner self. Let your genuine self come out—not only the self that you think others would approve of.

Keep the promises you've made to yourself, and keep the commitments you've made to others. Realistically appraise what promises you can make that you will keep and that you will have the energy to carry out.

Live according to your principles. The old virtues of telling the truth and doing what you say you'll do still go a long way. Refuse to compromise your values, and be defiant if necessary to preserve them. Live an ethical life that is worthy of you and that others can look to as a model.

BE AS SENSUAL AND PASSIONATE AS YOU CAN

Ageist views expect us to be dried-up prunes without vitality, sensuality, or sexuality. Happily, we are proving them wrong. Harold Ickes, the secretary of the interior under Franklin Roosevelt, fathered a child in his eighties.

Most of us have sexual feelings and experiences in later life. Find the ones that are possible and pleasurable for you. It isn't "performance" that's so important, but the sensual expressions of tenderness.

Sing along with William Butler Yeats:

> *You think it horrible that lust and rage*
> *Should dance attention upon my old age;*
> *They were not such a plague when I was young;*
> *What else have I to spur me into song?*

ACCEPT WHAT IS

Accept what is now irreversible in your life. By "acceptance," I mean what Avis Carlson means: "Acceptance is saying, 'Yes, I am growing older. It is happening now, today, and will continue to happen. I am grateful for the chance to experience it and the new opportunities it brings.'"[26]

Learn how to give up the things that matter to you as you begin to lose them—for example, an old house. In this way, you will be able to mourn and accept losses as they continue to occur.

Accept the leavings in life when you must, and pursue the grand prize when you can.

Resentment at your aging can worsen your infirmities; acceptance can temper and ease them.

COME TO TERMS WITH YOUR OWN MORTALITY

I have not fully absorbed the thought or the feeling that eventually everything dies, as Thomas Mann has: "The only religious way in which to regard death is to perceive and feel it as a constituent part of life, as life's holy prerequisite."[27]

---

26 Avis Carlson, *In the Fullness of Time* (Chicago: Contemporary Books, Inc., 1977), 132-133.
27 Thomas Mann, *The Magic Mountain*, trans. by John E. Woods (New York: Vintage, 1996), 237.

But now, in later life, the issue burrows deep in my gut, demanding that I come to terms with it. My most important challenge is to see my death as a natural development of my life—to determine the ways I would like to react to my dying, and then hope to die with surrender and inner peace.

By coming to a satisfactory resolution in our imagination about death, we may discover greater freedom in our current life. By coming to terms with the inevitability of our death, we might be freer to live more fully and pursue our goals more energetically.

I believe that to age well, we must adopt a stance toward death. The stance may vary from unconcern because we believe in an afterlife, to ignoring the issue until it can no longer be avoided, to trying to come to terms now with death and our fear of dying. One way to do it is by asking ourselves several questions in the hope that exploring them might help us emotionally accept death as the last phase of life.

What would be the way you would like to die, when you do? Is there something you can learn about death and dying that would be helpful to you? Do you want to think about it now, or later? Do you want to think about it occasionally and then forget it, or consider it in a more sustained way? Do you wish to avoid such thoughts completely, or just avoid getting preoccupied with them? Is there anything you want to do to prepare for your death? Can you contemplate your own death, then accommodate to it, and finally accept your impending nonexistence and consider it an aspect of aging?

Could you find ways to let the reality of your own demise sink in deeply without your being excessively disturbed or preoccupied with it? Do you find that your conviction surrounding your inevitable end enables you to live more fully and value life more highly?

Through trying to answer these questions, we may be able to develop some acceptable detachment and come to terms with the eventuality of our own death. But if you find yourself getting distressed in the process, stop asking or answering these questions. Just let them lie below the surface of your consciousness.

NINE

Becoming the Best Person
You Can Be

> *[What should concern us is] the fulfill-*
> *ment of our potentialities for healthful*
> *behavioral and psychological growth,*
> *potentialities with which we are so gen-*
> *erously endowed and which we have so*
> *little understood.*
> —Ashley Montagu from *Growing Young*

The purpose of this chapter is to help you discover the person you were meant to be, and find ways of becoming that person. Somewhere within you are aspects of your character that lie fallow, unexpressed. These are potentialities waiting to be realized as part of you and your being in the world.

If you have already been working at becoming the best person you can be, your task may be incomplete. And if you haven't, I submit that the most important goal you can commit to is to become the best person possible. This means that you strive to be a mensch (a genuine human being). It also means that you seek inner transformation so that you know who you are and how you are. As a consequence of such knowledge, you might become a more authentic, integrated, whole person.

What does it mean to be a mensch? Leo Rosten, in *The Joys of Yiddish*, defines a mensch as "an upright, honorable, decent person" or "someone of consequence, someone to admire and emulate, someone of noble character . . . The key to being a real *mentsh* is nothing less than character: rectitude, dignity, a sense of what is right, responsible, decorous."[28]

Below are descriptions of a person I consider menschen:

> *Alice at eighty-six was a gentle, strong, and compassionate human being. She had a special quality of attending to me and being fully present when we were together. She gave me the feeling that I had her undivided attention. I felt I was worth listening to, merited her support, and was a worthy and worthwhile person. In her*

---

28 Leo Rosten, *The New Joys of Yiddish*. New York: Crown Publishers, 2001.

presence, I felt respected as a unique individual whose qualities were of special interest to her. I felt that while listening to me, she understood my feelings in some deep place in herself and was resonating with my words.

One experienced Alice as a person of considerable seriousness, great depth, and integrity. When troubled friends and the spouses of her patients—she was a psychotherapist—needed to talk to her because they were upset, she was always available. The wisdom and gentleness that she treated them with was a constant refrain when they spoke of their experience with her.

She was not an effusive person, though she had a quiet warmth that touched without overwhelming you. You felt supported but not exposed or made dependent. And the comfort and self-containment she exhibited was somehow infectious, so that in her presence your anxiety diminished and you felt more integrated and self-confident.

Because she was a refugee from Nazi Germany, Alice understood deeply the potential for evil in humankind. This made her eager and diligent in seeking out and encouraging the good in others. Because she had lived a long life,

*seeing and experiencing both directly and vi-
cariously the depths and heights of the human
condition, she could be deeply empathic with
others. Because of her skills as a psychotherapist,
she often could alleviate others' pain and anguish. She was especially attuned to the tragic
dimensions of human life and accepted them
with courage and dignity. When they struck her
personally, she went on working, being helpful
to others right to the very end.*

By suggesting that you try to become a mensch,
I'm not proposing that you should expect to attain
some ideal state of awareness. Nor do I urge you to
become a saint. Rather, you should be able to derive
much gratification from each achievement that you
make, and from each step that you take in the direction of becoming the best person you can be.
And I predict that with each step forward, you will
improve the quality of your life, increase your satisfaction in living, and enhance your self-esteem and
self-respect.

Being a mensch and manifesting your positive
humanness often happens spontaneously in everyday life. It may suddenly come up in ways that are
difficult to fathom. At these times, you are probably not trying to "be a mensch." You didn't pursue

that objective self-consciously or purposefully. If you want to discover the ways this happens, it is important to reflect on the details of your daily life, learn from them, and use them as opportunities for expanding and deepening yourself. Any situation, event, or relationship is fair game for you to use in the growth and development of your character. You hear a moving piece of music; you are present at the birth of a child; someone close to you dies; you share a peak experience with an intimate; you are shaken by a frightening experience; you grapple with an emotional conflict that is difficult to resolve; you engage with a panhandler on the street; you are shaken by observing a family's poverty and suffering; your daughter gets married; you become a grandparent; you hear about someone's courageous or noble act, or participate in one yourself; you overcome a life-threatening illness; you win an award you have longed for; you lose a relationship that is important to you; you hear a speaker or see a play that inspires you; you read an author whose brilliance overwhelms you; you meet a person whose humanity touches you; you hear how the collective actions of a people brought about freedom, justice, and a better life. All these notable events, as well as the ordinary occurrences of everyday life, can be occasions for noticing their effect on your emotions, and their influence on your ways of thinking and behaving—for becoming more fully aware of how a new horizon has opened up for you. You can also reflect on the significance of these events for enlarging the scope of your awareness of your "self" and expanding your empathic capacities, honing your intuition, deepening your understanding of human nature, and gaining insight into the human condition.

But there will be times when you do not act like a mensch. It can be enlightening to scrutinize yourself at these times too. Were you indifferent to others, lacking in compassion, and concerned only about your own interests? Did you regard others only as objects that you might use? Did you engage in mean or thoughtless behavior? Did you abandon or forget about important commitments and responsibilities? Were you not entirely honest or trustworthy?

To change such less-than-menschlike behavior, you might examine your motivation and the reasons why you engage in such contrary behavior. And you may even discover how you can change.

Similarly, you can identify and reinforce those actions in which you engage others most positively. A good way to help you discover and reflect on these good acts is by asking yourself the right questions.

When, where, and how have you . . .

. . . empathized with and deeply understood another?

. . . felt that you acted with dignity, self-respect, and a sense of wholeness and integrity?

. . . taken a particularly life-affirming outlook or action?

. . . been concerned about, and acted for, the collective interest and the common good?

. . . sustained a deep, caring relationship with another?

. . . manifested a reverence for life either in your everyday activities or in a special situation?

. . . been particularly wise in making a difficult decision?

As with the previous chapter's discussion of the elements of aging well, there is no single key to being a good person. But there are some ways of being in the world that will make it easier.

CULTIVATING WISDOM

To know how to grow old is the master work of wisdom, and one of the most difficult chapters in the great art of living.
—Henri Frédéric Amiel from
Amiel's Journal: The Journal Intime of Henri-Frédéric Amiel,
translated by Mary A. Ward

Wisdom is one of the greatest gifts we can acquire and give to our loved ones and the world. We intuitively know what wisdom is, and we recognize when someone embodies it. Nevertheless, defining it might help our discussion.

Helen Luke describes it thus:

Now that the harvest is gathered and you stand in the autumn of your life, your oar is no longer a driving force carrying you over the oceans of your

*inner and outer worlds, but a spirit of discrim-
inating wisdom, separating moment by moment
the wheat of life from the chaff, so that you may
know in both wheat and chaff their meaning and
their value in the pattern of the universe.*[29]

Part of wisdom consists of being a model of thoughtfulness and deliberation before you act. It is a way of seeing
or viewing things with minimal distortion and maximum
objectivity. It is understanding human experience, especially how life is made meaningful. You demonstrate
wisdom in the way you *think*—in the accuracy of your
judgment, in the judiciousness of your evaluation, in the
incisive way you formulate and weigh an issue. You reveal
it in how you feel (with compassion, empathy, and intuition). You manifest it in "right conduct" by bringing
knowledge and morality to bear on an action. Wisdom
leads you to act in the interest of preserving, nourishing,
and adding to your own and others' well-being. With
wisdom, you carry on relationships that are mutually
caring, respectful, and preserving of your own and others'

---

29 Helen Luke, *Old Age: Journey Into Simplicity* (Great Barrington,
MA: Lindisfarne Books, 2010), 18.

self-esteem. Wisdom can also manifest in the way you speak, what you say, and the circumstances under which you openly express your opinion. You can demonstrate wisdom in whether and how you give advice and guidance, and the kind of counsel you give.

Ultimately, wisdom is a depth of understanding. Out of this understanding come actions that are morally enlightened and just, contribute to the development of others, foster a caring community, manifest a reverence for life, reflect an understanding of our interdependence with each other and the Earth, and preserve the various forms of life on the planet.

I am convinced that many of us know more, understand more, and have more wisdom than we are aware of. Therefore, I hope this discussion helps you unlock some of the wisdom inside you.

Wisdom is generally assumed to be a primary achievement of older age. Whatever the specific nature of that wisdom, the general idea is that accumulating long years of reflective experience gives us a deep understanding of the human condition and its foibles and virtues, and a better grasp of what to do to improve the human condition. Our wisdom enables us to become more fully developed, positive human beings and to enact higher standards of moral behavior.

Wise people teach the truth as they know it to others. They find vehicles for spreading their wisdom so that others may benefit from it. They are wise in dealing with themselves, especially their own aging, and in sharing that wisdom with others so that together they might produce a collective wisdom that is greater than any individual's.

We tend to think of wisdom as something difficult to achieve. But we all have the potential for it and can use it to improve our lives. And happily, there are also ways to cultivate and deepen your wisdom.

You can listen to wise women and men and learn from them. Read books that contain wisdom. They are not hard to find. Introspect, especially about any suffering or crisis that has affected you deeply. Discuss with others the significant events in your life and try to find the teaching. Reflect on the transitions and changes in your life. What have they taught you? Examine the lives of wise people—especially their thoughts on how they reflected on their own life. Use all your powers of imagination, intuition, logic, sensitivity, and fantasy to divine what is a wise decision in a particular situation, and what wisdom is in general.

After participating in a situation or event that was powerful or transformative for you, ask:

- What impact did it have on you? On him, on her, on them? And how do you feel about it? *Why* do you feel that way?

- What does the event mean to you? How, and why, was it meaningful?

- What can the event teach you about a person's personality or role, or about the human condition?

- What kind of compassion or understanding did you or the other show? How was it absent or present? What effect did it have on you?

- What were the various forces—social, psychological, economic, personal, spiritual, or other—in making the experience what it was? How did these forces work together or pull apart?

- Did you reach each other's humanity? If so, what did that look like? If not, why did you ignore or miss it?

- Did it contribute in any way to your experiencing a bond with the others involved? What did that bond consist of? How did that happen?

- Did the experience contribute in any way to your growth or understanding of yourself, another, a relationship, human nature, or society?

- How open or closed were you to what happened?

- What enabled you to identify with the other? Or, conversely, what prevented you from identifying with the other?

- Did the perspective and orientation of others prove enlightening, stretch your imagination, open up new vistas, offer you new insights and ideas to think about? What can you say, right here and now, about these new ways of thinking and feeling?

- Did you discover anything about your own interaction: how well or poorly it works, and the conditions it works best in?

Wisdom comes in many forms and dimensions. These are the things that I believe constitute wisdom about yourself and about events and situations in everyday life.

WISDOM ABOUT YOURSELF

Increase your awareness of your inner dynamics and your outward behavior so that you know who you are. Develop yourself to become an authentic, integrated, whole person.

Learn to face the dark sides of yourself—the destructive, cynical, cruel, mean sides of yourself. To learn about these facets is the beginning of learning how *not* to act on these destructive impulses—and, perhaps, learning to control and change them. If we can become aware of the dual aspects of our being— that is, that we are both good and bad—this might enable us to be more affirming of our own life and others.

Recognize that your self-interest and individual benefit are ultimately tied to, and interdependent with, the common good. Embody a generosity of spirit, time, affection, and understanding in relating to and guiding others.

Differentiate between what you need, what you want, what you prefer, what you will put up with, what you cannot tolerate, and what is absolutely out of the question for you. In this way, you can make more discriminating choices in the kind of life you want to lead.

WISDOM IN ATTITUDE AND WORLDVIEW

Look at things from a long perspective, historically or developmentally. Look at them in depth—burrowing into the core of the matter.

Maintain an intuitive trust in the life process. This also means that you appreciate and understand the will to live, especially when things are in a distressed or weakened state. To repair such situations, call on this will to live. But also know that while it can persist to the last moments of life, the will to live cannot prevail at the end.

Expand your view and vision so that it includes you as part of nature and encompasses the understanding that all living things must die, that death is a natural sequel to life, and that human life renews itself in the continuity of generations. Thus, we are links in the chain of human existence.

View our current social organizations and institutions as only temporary arrangements in the evolution of humankind. Just because an arrangement exists doesn't mean it is the best or "right" one. Expand your horizon, stretch your imagination, to envision new forms of social, political, economic, and psychological connection and organization, especially those in which a caring community can be developed.

Recognize that few things, and fewer people, are all one thing. Not all is black and white—we need to identify the subtle shades of gray. Understand that life is lived in the details and the process, as well as in the big picture and the end result. Find the part in the whole, and the whole in the part, and how each contributes to the other.

Accept and learn to deal with the apparent contradiction that so much of life is accidental, unplanned for, and uncontrollable—and, on the other hand, that much is predictable and controllable and can be planned for and realized as anticipated. If we learn to see ourselves in context, we realize that this context has its own context, and so on. That is, things do not stand alone.

DEEPENING YOUR POSITIVE HUMANITY

Fulfilling your highest potential involves a lot more than just being wise. It also means that you express your humanness as fully as you can—that you try to increase its quality, range, and depth. I am concerned here with expanding the positive aspects of our humanity while recognizing full well that being human has its dark and destructive aspects.

Stretch your boundaries so that nothing human is alien to you. In this way, your empathy can grow to include the whole range of human emotions and experiences. And who knows? You might be able to see yourself as not so different from another person. You might discover that you are capable of feeling and thinking in similar ways to others who are different from you. You can thereby increase your identification with others and open yourself up to understanding human experiences in whatever form they take.

Take every opportunity to extend your compassion and develop a "good heart." This means that you do things that contribute to the welfare of others, that you respect them and care about them, that you preserve their dignity and oppose anything that would crush their spirit.

Seek out and embrace the human dimension in social life. Identify the ways in which our economic, political, and other societal organizations affect concrete human beings. Then ask whether, and how, these are life-preserving and life-enhancing.

Practice confirming others as valuable and unique human beings. In this way, you confirm their existence as fellow human beings. And in doing so, be present with them; that is, give them your full and undivided attention while in their presence.

Explore the nature of your own humanity. You might discover, as Harry Stack Sullivan did, that "everyone is much more simply human than unique," and thereby be encouraged to become more "simply human."[30]

Transcend your identity beyond your immediate group and experience. Develop an *all-human* identity, in which you see yourself as a member of a common humanity.

What is common to us human beings? What is recognized as uniquely and specifically human behavior? I have pondered the question and have come up with these characteristics of the human condition that we share, and which are our common humanity.

> **Our common origin and basic needs.** We all are born of women and initially need someone to nurture and care for us if we are to survive.

> **Our interdependence.** We need each other for continuing existence.

> **Our aloneness.** Despite our communication, relationships, group identifications, and

---

30 Harry Stack Sullivan, *Conceptions of Modern Psychiatry* (New York: W.W. Norton & Company, 1954), 96.

merging, we still are enclosed in our own experience, unable to convey it as we experience it, and unable to "take in" others' experiences as they undergo them. Once we have separated from our mother, we exist alone, no matter how many and what kinds of unions we forge.

Our limitations. We all must confront physical, psychic, and social limitations and come to terms with them, whether by avoidance, submission, rejection, acceptance, or accommodation. On the other hand, we all share the common capacity—at least temporarily—to transcend these limitations in some way.

Our vulnerabilities. We all are subject to accident, injury, illness, and the vicissitudes of what we call fate or chance. And we all have some capacity, however tenuous, to cope with the consequences of our vulnerabilities.

Our emotions. We all experience and express a range of similar emotions, although their intensity, breadth, and quality may be different.

Our use of language. We are language users, employing vocal sounds and written symbols constantly in everyday life, thinking with them, and fashioning our lives through them.

Our finitude. We all share a common fate: death. In some way, we all have to come to terms with the eventual fact of our own death and nothingness, and with the emotions attendant upon facing it. We may respond with anxiety and dread or with resignation and acceptance; fear may be muted or conspicuous; we may recognize and grapple with the issue or avoid and fail to resolve it, but it remains an underlying theme in our lives.

Our common responsibility for the human race. And this means taking care of the planet where every human lives.

And finally, we all share a common capacity to confirm another as a fellow member of the human community, that is, recognize and honor their humanity as fully as we do our own.

In sharing a common humanity, no one is beyond the pale. No one can be kicked out of the human family. We all are entitled to the dignity that comes with being a person.

And the fullness of my own humanity can be measured by the degree to which I can confirm any other as a fellow human being, including all others in a common humanity.

Barbara Meyerhoff quotes one of her interviewees in her book *Number Our Days*:

> *In old age, we got a chance to find out what a human being is, how we could be worthy of being human. You could find in yourself courage, and know you are vital. Then you are living on a different plane. To do this you got to use your brain, but that's not enough. The brain is combined with the soul . . . I don't think you could get to this understanding too young, but when you get to it, then you couldn't go before your time, because you are ready.[31]*

Of course, we can grow our humanity in a million ways. We might discuss with others a highly emotional event

---

31 Barbara Meyerhoff, *Number Our Days* (New York: Simon & Schuster, 1980), 198.

such as the birth or death of a child. Or we may be grappling with a physical illness or debility that another person also has. We become more human by participating in transitional events such as weddings and graduations, by traveling in cultures different from our own and experiencing the world from their point of view, by reading histories of when people's humanity rose to meet adversity, and just by meeting and engaging with people who have led very different lives from our own.

When you have a strong sense of our common humanity, you feel respect for everyone, and responsibility to preserve the entire human community. Your "I" becomes part of the "we," and your self interweaves with all the selves that constitute humankind.

Unfortunately, cultural, institutional, and personal prejudices and distortions get in the way of sharing our humanity. Thus, racism involves unconsciously or deliberately dehumanizing the other and not seeing him or her as a fellow human. Homophobia compels some of us to automatically exclude someone with a different sexual orientation from the human family and view them as somehow wrong or unworthy. Nationalism, especially in time of war, enables many of us to dehumanize the enemy so that we can kill them without the compunction we would feel at killing a human being like ourselves. All of these are instances of dehumanization.

MAKING A SPIRITUAL CONNECTION

As we grow older, most of us seek a deeper under-standing of the meaning of our existence. We become fascinated, intrigued, by the mysteries of birth, death, and our connection to the eternal.

Here's how Polly Francis expresses her sense of a spir-itual connection.

A new set of faculties seem to be coming into op-eration. I seem to be awakening to a larger world of wonderment—to catch little glimpses of the immensity and diversity of creation. More than at any other time in my life, I seem to be aware of the beauties of our spinning planet and the sky above. And now I have the time to enjoy them. I feel that old age sharpens our awareness. [32]

32 Polly Francis, "The Autumn of My Life," *Friends Journal,* November 1, 1975, 556.

Some of us believe that a fully developed human being necessarily leads a spiritual life, maintains a spiritual attitude and faith, or connects to what they consider the spiritual dimension. Many of us hunger for something beyond our ordinary realities—beyond the mundane, pragmatic, and scientific. We have a strong desire to feel reverence toward something or someone "higher" than ourselves. We want to be involved with matters of real concern. We might believe, with Toynbee, that "to be human is to be capable of transcending oneself."[33] We may feel that spiritual faith is a foundation for our ethical standards. Or we believe that a spiritual attitude is the basis for our life and explains our very existence.

Here is how Albert Einstein expressed his view of spirituality:

> *To know what is impenetrable to us really exists, manifesting itself as the highest wisdom and the most radiant beauty, which our dull faculties can comprehend only in the most primitive forms—this knowledge, this feeling, is at the*

---

33 Arnold Toynbee, *Experiences*. New York: Oxford University Press, 1969.

center of true religiousness. In this sense, and in this sense only, I belong to the ranks of devoutly religious men.[34]

As any who have tried know, to define or pin down what is spirituality is extremely difficult if not impossible. It is something we must contemplate and come to our own feeling about, even if—or especially if—that feeling is beyond words. John Neihardt offers:

"The exaltation of expanded awareness in moments of spiritual insight is good. This may occur in a flash, glorifying the world; or it may linger for days, when you seem to float above all worldly troubling, and all faces become familiar and dear. This state can be spontaneously generated, but it has often been achieved through fasting and prayer."[35]

---

34 Albert Einstein, *Living Philosophies* (New York: Simon & Schuster, 1931), 7.
35 John Neihardt, *The Giving Earth: A John G. Neihardt Reader* (Lincoln, NE: University of Nebraska Press, 1991), 271.

Mary Ann, who is seventy-three, told me that she ages well by maintaining a relationship with God. He looks after her and enables her to do good and be good. This special relationship with God helps her live in a positive way and pulls her through occasional depressions. She keeps her relationship with God, and her beliefs about rebirth, quite private, and they have a sustaining power for her.

Many people have undertaken meditation as a way of connecting with the sacred. Meditation gives them a sense of the unifying energy in the universe, bringing them inner peace and a more harmonious relationship with the planet.

Followers of various faiths seek to do good by sanctifying everyday life, by interacting with others honestly, compassionately, and with loving kindness. But the definition of "good" varies widely and is viewed differently by adherents of different religious groups. Some religious groups preach guilt, shame, and bigotry. It is important that we find a spirituality that promotes well-being and wisdom for ourselves and others, instead of insisting that our spiritual beliefs are the only truth.

The test of your spirituality is how it works in your life. Whatever the nature of your spiritual commitment, the issue is always how you apply your spiritual practice every day, how you sanctify your mundane activities, how you venerate the ongoing moment and seek what is holy in your daily living. Are some places, things, and people sacred for you? Do you honor and respect all others and see the potential in them that might be evoked and realized?

What does sanctifying everyday life mean to you? Does your spirituality encourage you to feel and think and act as if you share a common humanity with all others, and to enhance the quality of their lives? And does it help you see yourself as an interdependent part of nature?

If matters of the spirit were to infuse matters of the concrete, material world, they might indeed bring about a transformation in the ways we live with ourselves, each other, and our physical and social environment.

CONTRIBUTING TO THE PRESENT AND THE FUTURE

Many of us in later life would like to reach into the future, make some mark in it, live on in it, and leave a legacy after we are gone, as a way of fulfilling our potential. For most of us, our children and grandchildren constitute our greatest contribution to the future.

Some of us also wish to contribute to the future and be remembered in it in a particular way, to influence the shape it takes and the values that prevail. There are many ways we can accomplish this goal.

We can, for example, become role models and mentors for people younger than we are. Peter Ustinov tells us, "The young need old men. They need men who are not ashamed of age, not pathetic imitations of themselves."[36] We can reflect humanitarian principles, moral stances, and actions that support just causes. We can raise the level of consciousness about the human potential, and we can help individuals realize their own potential.

The degree to which you manifest wisdom, humanness, and spirituality in your life is the degree to which you can serve as a role model for younger people to become menschen themselves.

Rather than emphasize competition as our default mode of behavior, we need to make cooperation and collaboration our primary way of relating to each other. We need to share our abundance, rather than hoard it for ourselves. We need to see our self-interest and the common good as complementary and mutually reinforcing, rather than at odds.

---

36 John Lahr, "Ustinov's Many Lives," *New York Times*, September 25, 1977, 266.

By the ways in which we act wisely and spiritually, we can contribute to a new vision of what is possible in later life. We can demonstrate and affirm that our lives can be transformative. We can find continual meaning and self-improvement, as well as contribute to the common good in our society. We can project new possibilities in later life—possibilities that we could not contemplate or were afraid even to imagine. We need only awaken and mobilize the resources that are already here, inside us, in others, and in our society.

AFTERWORD

My father has remained a vibrant presence in my life long after his passing in 1995. This project, editing Dad's words, has enhanced that feeling and focused my attention on a special time for Dad and me.

It was the spring of 1989. I had just returned to Boston from an eighteen-month backpacking haul around Asia that included a hitching stint in the remote Western Tibet/Mt. Kailas region. The trip was a point of no small tension between the family and me because of my inability to contact them. Dad even refers to his fears around my Tibet adventure in chapter four of this book.

Dad, a professor of sociology with an emphasis on mental health, had been made emeritus (which, he joked, meant "without merit") by Brandeis University. A keen observer of society by trade, he was troubled by how elderly people were marginalized and made to feel less than those of fewer years. He was even more bothered by the fact that elderly people internalized these feelings of being useless and lived out their final years in quiet pathos. He was determined to reach other people and offer an avenue to make the twilight the most incandescent light in people's lives. Dad decided to write a book.

Dad had already made this decision by the time I dropped my tattered backpack and washed off the Tibetan dust and Indian gravel at the house on the short, quiet street on the West Newton hill. He was deeply into outlining his ideas, writing chapters, and pushing himself to take initial thoughts further. Thus, it was pure serendipity that my four-month hiatus between traveling in Asia and moving to Japan coincided with my father's most fertile period in writing this work. Dad and I were able to hang out and discuss his thoughts. It was an unusual time for me in that I had neither a job to attend to nor the call of the enigmatic East to heed. No doubt Dad was amused to have a much younger person as a sounding board for a manuscript on aging.

Dad felt a responsibility to try to help others celebrate their aging. He also saw the book as a wonderful opportunity to synthesize many of the ideas he had been talking about in his classes and therapeutic practice. (In addition to teaching, Dad offered therapy at a low-cost/free center he cofounded in Cambridge, Massachusetts, called Greenhouse.) These ideas ranged from how to "stay human" to how to stay engaged in life, how to continue to learn, how to remain involved in your community, and how to stay related to people, among others.

During 1988 to 1992, Dad concentrated on this writing and was very productive. After he was done with the manuscript, it seems the ALS started to touch him, and focus on the book diminished.

When I rediscovered the manuscript, Mother was extremely supportive but also quite exacting. We discussed at length how and why to edit the writing. This process was quite lengthy as I was living in Japan and visiting Boston only periodically. Dad had a myriad of influences, which sometimes led to many ideas being crammed together. He liked to be all-inclusive, so sometimes inventories of ideas became unwieldy. Editing would be essential.

Mom was perfectly qualified to help me. We had often talked about and explored how she edited and rewrote with my dad on his first two great academic books, *The Mental Hospital* (1954) and *The Nurse and the Mental Patient* (1956). She also coauthored the book *Social Approaches to Mental Patient Care* (1964) with him.

The Mental Hospital was Dad's watershed work. Written with then-renowned psychiatrist Alfred H. Stanton, the monograph detailed how the environment; the relationships between the doctors, nurses, and staff;

and their particular interests could have a profound effect on the psychiatric patients in a care facility.

The book made Dad such a luminary in the fields of social psychology and sociology that Brandeis offered him a tenured full professorship to start at the institution. The work influenced a generation of caregivers and pushed the fields forward, toward a more humanitarian view of the patient. I had always thought that it took Dad some time to present his second academic monograph, *The Nurse and the Mental Patient*, but in fact, that wasn't the case. Two years later, that work made an impact in the psychiatric world, specifically addressing the role of the nurse, and how he or she might better interact with a patient.

Mom played a major part in all of Dad's academic writing and had numerous publications from her own research. Starting in 1968, she had a position at the Psychiatric Clinic at MIT. She wrote or cowrote, with renowned psychiatrist Merton Kahne, a myriad of papers in the field. So, in addition to being intimately familiar with Dad's thought, Mother was well qualified and experienced professionally to advise me on the editing of the text.

The process has been long but enjoyable. I'm confident that Dad, in his study in 1989, would have been extremely pleased this work is finally available. Remember Dad's mantra: Stay Human!

—Rob Schwartz, June
2021, Brookline, MA

APPENDIX

Caring Communities

Of course, it's not enough to be concerned about ourselves alone and pursue our own self-interest exclusively. For our own well-being and survival, we must contribute to the common good and to the interest of the collectivity. For if the society breaks down, we will suffer many forms of injury, and our very survival may be threatened.

One of the most important ways of becoming the best person you can be is to devote yourself to creating, participating in, and maintaining a caring community.

A caring community can be created in almost any social context. Its central features are mutual respect and concern, serious consideration of one another's opinions, a shared common concern and purpose, and the dedication of each member to the interests of the collectivity. In a caring community, people work together to achieve common goals and to benefit both the collectivity and themselves individually.

Thus, you can create a caring community with your friends, your family, your neighbors, your local community. At the global level, you can join organizations such as Greenpeace, the Audubon Society, or the African Wildlife Foundation, which are working to protect the environment. You can work in these organizations to maintain a caring community within them, as well as try to further their global objectives.

Aside from our individual actions, we can participate in collective action with like-minded people, both young and old, who share our determination to bring about the social changes that will help create a caring community. If you believe as I do, that our society, though in better shape than many others, is in a state of moral decline, then you may be inclined to join with others and contribute to societal repair and transformation. With so much destructiveness all around, it is our obligation to be constructive, to work for a more just economic, social, and political order and for the preservation and protection of the planet. We can try, with our collective wisdom and action, to assert our power to lead the nation out of its systemic dysfunctions, its cynicism, its divisive inequality, its enraging injustices, its daily distortions, its assaults on the truth, its endemic prejudices, and its arrogance toward the multiple planetary perils that already beset us. By collective transformative action, we can contribute to a caring community and to the continuity of the human species and feel ourselves to be positive links in the great chain of being.

There are many valid ways to create and participate in caring communities. If you don't have access to such organized, humane communities, you can work toward creating them for yourself and your loved ones. In the meantime, we can also work to expand our networks of care and support so that our lives can be as full of the nurturance and love and growth as we desire.

This section will not be a survey of all the ways that diverse cultures over time have built caring communities for people in later life. But it will give examples of existing communities, to provide a glimpse of what is possible, both in the long run and right now, today. I hope it will provide food for your imagination and inspire you to work toward creating a caring community in your own life.

THE CENTER FOR CREATIVE RETIREMENT

The Center for Creative Retirement is one such community. As the name suggests, it provides meaningful opportunities for adults of retirement age to use their skills and abilities. It provides avenues for elders to volunteer in their community, participate in civic activities, enhance their education, and pursue wide-ranging interests. The center draws on the huge bank of skills that older people possess, and puts them to use where they are sorely needed: in the local community. It's worth noting that this community could exist just as well in any similar-sized city in the United States.

The following excerpt comes from the July 14, 1991, issue of *Parade:*

In Asheville, NC, people don't worry about what to do after they retire. Here, they see age as an asset.

Recently I traveled to Asheville, NC, and met some of the community's leading citizens. Carolyn Rosenthal found time for me in between meetings of the reading groups she runs in the area. Earl Hitchcock squeezed me in during a busy day of administering a volunteer program. I tracked down Bob Etter in his physical chemistry lab and went to an inner-city school to find Mel Hetland and

Evelyn Smith. Bob and Peggy Tinkler had a little more free time; they had just finished work on a grueling political campaign and were settling back into their more normal routines as college students.

This was not a collection of native Ashevilleans—nor did they have much else in common. By training, they were a dancer, a businessman, a corporate research director, two educators, an insurance man, and a travel agent. Some had lived in the upper Midwest and the Northeast; one had spent his career in places like Saigon and Buenos Aires. All had, at the age of 65 or so, wound down their primary careers. The rest of the world would call them retired.

Asheville calls them leaders.

Approximately 13 percent of this country's citizens—around 32 million people—are 65 or older. Although no exact statistics are kept, experts believe that most of these individuals are in good health. Life expectancies for Americans vary by sex, race and other demographic factors, but many older people today can expect to live into their eighties. And in 30 years, as many members of the Baby Boom generation are reaching retirement age, the number of older Americans will start to rise by 50 percent.

Statistics like these led the University of North Carolina at Asheville to set up its North Carolina Center for Creative Retirement. "Until recently, most of the nation's concern for senior citizens was concentrated on the frail, the fragile and the impoverished," said Ronald J. Manheimer, the center's director. "Those people are very important. But other seniors were ignored."

With its reasonable cost of living, temperate climate and breathtaking view of the Blue Ridge Mountains, Asheville has grown increasingly popular as a place for older people: 16,000 of the city's 62,000 residents are retirees. About 1,500 of those participate each year in the programs of the Center for Creative Retirement. In the center's noncredit College for Seniors, retirees can further their education. In its Senior Academy for Intergenerational Learning, they can pass on their knowledge to young people. Through Leadership Asheville

Seniors, they work in the schools, hospital and prisons of the community.

In Asheville, "retired" people are running discussion groups for adults in rural communities; helping hospitals, libraries and orchestras to organize their finances and marketing; and counseling college students on career choices. "These are people of talent—resourceful, bright and capable," said Ron Manheimer. "They had been an untapped resource."

The older people who take part in the center's programs live in their own homes and commute to their jobs and classes on and off campus. Some might spend as little as two hours a week taking a course in poetry or physics or arms control at the College for Seniors. Others spend all or part of almost every weekday working on center-sponsored projects. "You don't see many people withering away or floundering around for something to do around here," Bob Tinkler, 67, told me.

Earl Hitchcock, 72, certainly wasn't floundering around when I met with him. "I've got my hands full," he said cheerfully, gesturing at a thick pile of paperwork. A few years ago,

Hitchcock was a businessman in New Jersey. Today, he coordinates the work of 80 volunteers in the public schools of the Asheville area. "When I retired, I didn't have anything specific in mind that I wanted to do," Hitchcock said. "I knew I wanted to play tennis—and I've done that. But my wife and I had always been active in the community—United Way, Cub Scouts, a family-counseling service—and we wanted to remain active."

Hitchcock attended the seven-week Leadership Asheville Seniors training course, in which political, educational and philanthropic leaders taught the participants about the community's needs. "They talked about drug addiction, dropouts, the usual litany of city problems. It occurred to us that every one of these problems was education-related."

Hitchcock and other members of his class worked together with area principals to bring older people into the public schools, matching them with students who needed tutors, remedial help or just an adult to talk to. One elderly volunteer tutored a young girl who had been through four foster homes in one school year. She knitted the girl a sweater, helped her with reading and gave her a shoulder to cry on. Another volunteer helped a grade-school student who had been failing math, and the child scored an 85 on a math exam. "Some people said that seniors wouldn't be interested in schools, because they don't have kids in school anymore," Hitchcock said. "But absolutely nobody we talked to felt that way."

For Mel Hetland, 70, the center offers a very special way to serve his community while keeping his hand in the profession he loves. Hetland is one of a small group of volunteers from the center who work at Randolph Elementary School, in a downtrodden section of Asheville. Once a week, he teaches reading to first- and third-graders and devises science demonstrations for fifth-graders. "The big reward is that I'm helping some teacher develop techniques that I had a lot of experience with during my own career as a curriculum supervisor and professor of education," he said.

In a laboratory at the University of North Carolina at Asheville, Prof. John Stevens and his students have been doing research on the

Mossbauer effect—a nuclear technique that scientists use to study the structure of matter. Stevens has spent much of his career in this work and has introduced hundreds of eager undergraduates to research. Since last summer, he has been grouping his young students with people from the center. "It's been one of the most fruitful semesters I've had in 20 years of research," he said.

Bob Etter, 58, and Terri Spangler, 21, have begun a remarkable partnership. Bob, who has a Ph.D. in chemistry, retired two years ago as research vice president of Johnson's Wax; Terri is a UNC-Asheville junior. "I was expecting to be of service when I retired," Bob said. "I do a lot of volunteer things. But this is the only one I've found in which I can use my scientific background." Working as a team, Bob and Terri run painstaking analyses on specialized equipment, which they learn about as they work together.

The undergraduates in the program admit that they were apprehensive at first about having retired scientists looking over their shoulders. Now, though, Terri pays the program the ultimate compliment: "It's the kind of thing I'd like to do when I retire," she says.

You don't need to be a scientist or a business leader to benefit from the center. "Some of the smartest people in our classes only got as far as high school," said one College for Seniors participant. Carolyn Rosenthal, 67, a former librarian from New York City and Washington, DC, has started a reading discussion group for adults in rural communities around Asheville. "At first," she recalled, "I had to convince them that they could be members of a reading group. Now a lot of these people are candidates for courses at the College for Seniors."

Today, the scope of the North Carolina Center for Creative Retirement makes it one of a kind, but Ron Manheimer believes that other creative retirement centers could spring up around the country. With a budget of about $350,000—which comes in part from the university, foundation grants and the fees of its students—the center has relatively low costs. "The programs are replicable, if you have dedicated people," said Manheimer.

Already, consultants from retirement communities and government have come to study the center. The White House named it one of President Bush's 1,000 Points of Light. Manheimer concedes that the Center for Creative Retirement is not for everyone; some people lead rich, happy retired lives just puttering in the garden, playing golf and visiting with the grandchildren. But retired people everywhere can learn an important lesson from its philosophy. As Earl Hitchcock put it: "If you can't think of anything to do when you retire, you don't have much imagination."[37]

FINDHORN GARDEN

Findhorn Garden, in Scotland, is a highly organized spiritual community of about three hundred members who hail from more than a dozen countries. Unlike the Center for Creative Retirement, it includes people of all ages, from infants to octogenarians, all drawn

---

37 Michael Ryan, "Here, They See Age as an Asset," *Parade*, July 14, 1991, 4-5.

together for a common purpose. Findhorn members devote themselves to a number of gardens, which they nurture along with their spiritual lives. It is a place that leaves few visitors unchanged. Healing themselves, each other, and the earth are the driving forces behind their endeavor, and if their gardens are any evidence, they're doing something right.

The *Mother Earth News* adds the following:

> . . . Even in the garden school, which offers a three month course of study, tries to provide a learning environment where staff grow food and flowers, and most important, themselves. As Eileen's advisory voice has pointed out, people come first.
>
> In a world that normally places more important on such things as economics, "the job," material possessions, political power, and being "right" than on a person's deep inner need for love and acceptance, this simple and sane attitude is wonderfully refreshing . . .
>
> Physically, the community now embraces

over half the caravan park, numerous bungalows, two manor houses and one mansion (with a combined 15 acres of grounds), an old railway station, and the stewardship of the Hebridean island of Erraid . . . and in 1975 (as Eileen's voice of guidance had long predicted) the Findhorn Foundation *bought* the Cluny Hill Hotel—which is now called Cluny Hill College—and used it to house an education program that draws some 5,000 guests annually.

Though the average stay for Findhorn members is now three years, the community has always seen itself as a seedbed from which new concepts of society and civilization would be transplanted *throughout* the earth. Even Eileen, Peter and Dorothy are no longer in permanent residence. As early as 1971, Eileen's inner voice told her that folks were depending too much on her advice, and its last message to the community was, "Go within, and find your own guidance." Dorothy left in 1973 for her native Canada, where she helped establish the Loran Association.

At present (though change is practically a

Findhorn password), the community's three main governmental branches are Administration, Education, and Focalizers and Community. The "focalizers" are the managers of some 37 departments, who say that they focus (rather than dictate) the energies of the people in their given areas, "like water through a funnel." And the primary tools used to keep every one's energies properly channeled are called "attunements" . . . brief moments (or longer sessions if a major problem or disagreement exists) when department members hold hands, close their eyes, and experience a "coming together" of the group and the task it faces.

The effectiveness of this method is demonstrated in many ways. It's reflected in the bimonthly magazine, *One*, and the fine books and tapes produced by Findhorn publication and audiovisual centers, in the sparkling clean radiance that permeates the community's buildings, in meals featuring an incredible variety of healthful, tasty fare, in the "networking" that the communication center constantly maintains with planetary communities and happenings all over the world, and in the warm openness of the guest focalizers, who make strangers feel instantly at ease.

Equally impressive are the members' quick smiles and child-bright eyes, the laughter that bubbles like bird song across the community, the minimum of dogma and rules, the exciting exploration of new and ancient ways of relating to the planet and its beings, the humor poked at typical New Age stuffiness and jargon, and—perhaps best of all—the conversations that make you realize the superficial levels upon which humankind usually communicates.

Findhorn, while *not* a utopia, certainly is—at the very least—a dynamic place to pursue the unfolding of an individual personality in a supportive and joyful group context.[38]

---

38 "Findhorn Foundation: A Bright Light in a Dark World," *Mother Earth News*, published September 1, 1981, https://www.motherearthnews.com/sustainable-living/nature-and-environment/findhorn-foundation-zmaz81sozraw/

THE UNIVERSITY FOR THE AGED

China has a long-standing tradition of respect for the elderly. This community enables people in later life to return to school and not only continue their formal education but also develop talents that may have lain dormant for a lifetime. And they can do it in the company of other motivated older people. This article appeared in the *New York Times*.

AT 102, HE'S BACK IN SCHOOL, WITH MANY LIKE HIM

Qian Likun is a model university student, the kind of diligent scholar-athlete who joins in foot races, excels in his studies and is never distracted by a woman's short skirt.

Mr. Qian is also five times older than most university students. He is 102 years old, and while ordinary students study the Boxer Rebellion of 1900 and the fall of the Ching Dynasty in 1911, Mr. Qian has no such problem: he remembers them.

The University for the Aged, where Mr. Qian studies, has 8,000 students here in Wuhan, a major city on the Yangtze River of central China. Founded five years ago, it is part of a network of more than 800 such institutions for the elderly in China, all founded in the last eight years.

China has traditionally revered the aged, and this nation's programs for the elderly are very impressive for a developing country. Some Chinese villages have a special "house for the aged," where senior citizens can live if they have no children to depend on, and most cities have a range of physical fitness, entertainment and educational programs for retired citizens.

Questions for the U.S.

One question that Chinese often ask Americans is why families sometimes put their parents in institutions, why such a rich country cannot do more for its elderly. The questions include a hint of reproach, but mostly wonder at the breach of filial piety.

"We want to help the elderly help themselves, so that they can reduce their dependence on their families and on society," said Lu Jianye, the vice president of the Wuhan University for the Aged. "We also want to help them increase their contribution to society, and to develop hobbies such as art, calligraphy or even massage, so that they can enjoy their later years."

The university here, which charges tuition of less than $5 a term, offers courses in 123 subjects. These include painting, disco dancing, calligraphy, bridge, cooking, English, literature and health care for the elderly.

Canes Beside the Chairs

Most people in Wuhan are literate, but the university also arranges classes in some neighborhoods to teach reading and writing to the elderly, mostly women who never went to school.

China, with a population of 1.1 billion, has some 115 million people over the retirement age, which is normally 60 for men and 55 for women. The proportion of the aged will rise sharply in coming decades as baby boom generations grow older and family planning policies reduce the number of young people.

On a recent visit, the classrooms of the Wuhan University for the Aged were full of animated students, some with canes beside their chairs, enthusiastically commenting on each other's paintings, reciting standard phrases of English and dissecting ancient poetry.

"We don't want to get senile," said Yan Bin, a 56-year-old woman who retired recently as a professional singer. She was sitting around a table with three partners, working on her skills at bridge, the card game favored by Deng Xiaoping and countless other elderly Chinese.

"I never studied bridge before," said Mu Youqing, a silver-haired woman of 64 years who is a retired doctor. "But it's very highbrow and cultured, and it has a long history in China."

A Boost for the Brain

The baby of the foursome, 56-year-old Shao Kanfu, a lean, tall man who retired early, added, "I wanted to look after my health and give my brain a boost."

Most elderly people in China live with their children, and often they are responsible for caring for their grandchildren. So the University for the Aged holds classes in the midmorning and again in the early afternoon, when the students' children are at work and their grandchildren are at school.

In addition, because some of the old people cannot get around easily, the university has set up 13 branches around the city in residential areas. The university depends for money on tuition fees and also on generous grants from the city government. The faculty consists mostly of professors at nearby universities who are delighted to moonlight for a small fee.

"The teaching level isn't as high as at a regular university, and we don't go into as much depth as we would with younger students," said Zhou Wu, a junior high school instructor who teaches Chinese literature on the side at a branch campus of the University for the Aged. "But some of the older folks bring a good deal of enthusiasm as well as diverse experience to the classroom, so it's often more interesting to teach them than to teach my regular students."

Along for the "Fun Run"

One of Mr. Zhou's most diligent students is Mr. Qian, the 102-year-old. A retired agricultural researcher, Qian diligently prepares for each class session and offers some pointed views.

"This poem isn't very good by Tang Dynasty standards," he said the other day as Mr. Zhou dissected a poem on the blackboard. "But it's better than anything we have today."

Mr. Qian manages to walk to the class on his own, and he hears and sees well enough to follow the teacher most of the time. The first class he took was on health care for the elderly, and he says he found it very useful in looking after his wife, who died a few months ago at the age of 100, and his daughter, who is 81 years old and in fading health.

When the university held a "fun run" this spring, some 300 old people ran about 2.3 miles to complete the race. Mr. Qian was among them, but the university staff acknowledges that his pace was more of a hobble than a jog.

A lover of traditional poetry, Mr. Qian scarcely paused when asked for a few lines of his favorite poem. The room fell silent as he recited from memory this ancient Chinese poem:

> *The clouds are wispy this morning,*
> *the breeze is light.*
> *As I pass the pond, I see flowers*
> *and willow trees.*
> *The passers-by don't know the joy in my heart.*
> *I'm like a kid at play.*[39]

HUMAN, ALWAYS HUMAN

This final example of a caring community is different from the previous three in a very significant way: it is entirely noninstitutional. It is the caring community that one person created for himself over the course of

---

39 Nicholas D. Kristof, "At 102, He's Back in School, With So Many Like Him," *New York Times*, December 6, 1990, A4.

a lifetime. Many of us have created this type of supportive and mutually enriching network, and all of us can enhance our personal circles of connection and relationships. By giving to others as well as taking care of himself, David has nurtured a caring community worthy of admiration and emulation.

David, who is eighty-six years old, is a truly extraordinary person. Yet many ordinary people, particularly women, have created similar types of caring communities around themselves. David's "good deeds" are usually spontaneous, impulsive, and uncalculated activities, in which he gives to others and validates them as worthwhile human beings. Although his actions are spontaneous, they are also intended in the sense that he generally wishes to do good things and be kind to other people.

David has spent over forty years working for his local community. He has worked hard for a number of causes, such as rent control and smaller classes in the schools of that community. He has also worked many years on grassroots organizing.

David has a way of converting an impersonal initial encounter into an interhuman relationship. He is not content to let someone who approaches him on the street remain anonymous and in his role. He will immediately engage this person in a human exchange, asking in a sincere, warm voice, "Where do you come from?

Why are you doing this work? Do you like it? How long have you been doing it?" Within a few minutes, the interchange is not between two strangers, but between two people who treat each other with respect, have a good feeling between them, and leave the interaction feeling good about themselves and each other. Similarly, when David is traveling by train, here and abroad, he strikes up conversations with the person in the seat next to him. By the time the trip is over, David has often made a friend of that person, in some instances keeping that friendship for the rest of his life, even hosting them in his home and being a guest in theirs.

In the same way, he makes a friend and confidante of his housekeeper. He also does this with his students. Over the years, many have become his friends, and he keeps up a lively and continuing correspondence with them. He has taken many individuals and couples into his house, offering them his upstairs apartment free of charge. One of these people, many years after his tenure in David's house, flew in from Germany to stay when David was incapacitated from a bad accident. He stayed with David a few weeks, and when he was ready to leave, the friend offered to quit his job if David needed him. David inspires this kind of love and devotion in his friends. In the same fashion, a young couple living in the upstairs apartment quickly became like his adopted children, and he like a father to them. They took very loving and tender care of him every day.

He devotes himself to others, so they devote themselves to him. He is open to them, and they open up to him. He cares about them and treats them with warmth and affection, and they reciprocate. He keeps his friendships alive, corresponding with over a hundred people. He asks people to keep in touch with him and to visit, and shows his joy and appreciation when they do. He exudes sincerity and gentleness and draws people to him because they experience his lack of pretense and his genuine interest in them. They also feel unthreatened and important in his presence. And most importantly, he respects each of them as a fellow human being. For David, there are no superficial contacts, and he is impulsive with his generosity toward others. With these many widespread relationships in his local community and all over the world, David has created a dispersed caring community, with him as its center.

In addition to all these friendships, he has close family relationships with several siblings, nephews, and nieces. One nephew in particular is an ever-present helper who keeps a sharp eye out for David's welfare.

When I asked him in an interview what advice he would offer young people, he said, "Follow your heart and learn from experience." What accounts for the deep human relationships he has made? "I realize that

I share a common humanity with all other people. I don't puff myself up and feel better than anyone else. I am anti-snobbish." He went on to say that he takes a nonjudgmental attitude toward others, which helps him understand them. He wants to be helpful to others because he himself has had many difficult experiences that he had to overcome. He therefore has deep sympathy with what people have to go through in life and for the suffering that people must endure as part of the human condition. He says, "I've always had a feeling for the underdog. I am curious and intrigued by other people and the plot of their lives. I have the feeling that most people feel alone and have little confidence in themselves. At the same time, they have special qualities which need to be brought home to them, to make up for the lacks they have. I derive this from the fact that I lacked self-confidence when I was young. I was insecure. This evokes identification and sympathy. I have the responsibility, if it is in my power, to help supplement the lacks in people's lives. This is the price I should pay for the pleasure I get from the association with so many wonderful people. I delight in the company of others. I sometimes wonder how much of it is a desire to have them like me. The longer I live, the more I realize how fortunate I am, and I feel that I should share my good fortune. The older I am, the more suffering I see. My capacity for feeling deeper grows. I am amazed I still have the intensity."

David goes on to tell me, "I hang on to people and I encourage people to hang on to me, by my continued interest in them." David is always asking himself, "How can I be helpful?" For example, he hears that a foreign student needs a place to stay, and David offers his home. Sometimes they stay a few days, sometimes a few months. David goes on to explain, "I just like people. I feel for their problems. I like doing things for them. I suspect that part of my motivation is to curry favor. It results in other people loving me and keeping in touch. I think it's because I want to be different than my father. Money was the central thing in his life. But I take after my mother, who was kind, gentle, understanding, and down-to-earth. I used to have the feeling (when I was younger) that I wasn't such a nice person or a lovable one. So I may be overcompensating for that."

When I pressed David to tell me how he viewed himself, he said, "I don't set time aside to appraise myself. I see myself as a nice person, decent, generous, knowledgeable, impetuous, undisciplined, spoiled, but I don't have an inflated notion of my own value." He also confessed that he thinks of himself as a mensch, who, by his definition, is someone who has the ability to get close to people. It took him until his thirties, when he married, to arrive at that point. He says, "Being a mensch means to me, to live up to my ideals of honesty, decency, and good social relations, not lying, and not being a greedy pig. However, I think I have the potential for being a hypocrite. I am tempted to do things I shouldn't. Then I see that it's just childishness, to do something unacceptable and be scolded for it. So, I usually hew to a good moral line."

All in all, David's genuine love of people and interest in them has led him to expand his circle to a point that is truly life-enhancing.

The caring communities we have discussed represent four out of many, each of them like no other. Some caring communities are institutionalized, while others are organic. Some are based on a shared philosophy or cause, while others revolve around a shared desire to learn or give to others. Each in its own way, if it is truly a caring community, provides for its participants a sense of meaning and connection, as well as an avenue for giving back to others something of what life has given us. If the whole world were set up in caring communities, I can only imagine what an awe-inspiring vision of humanity we would realize.